The
espresso
Bible

The
espresso
Bible
The Bible in sips

David Winter

LION

Text copyright © 2007 David Winter
Bible extracts are taken from the
Contemporary English Version and are
used by permission of the Bible Society
and HarperCollins Publishers. Full CEV text
is available from www.bibleresources.org.uk.

The author asserts the moral right
to be identified as the author of this work

A Lion Book
an imprint of
Lion Hudson plc
Mayfield House, 256 Banbury Road,
Oxford OX2 7DH, England
www.lionhudson.com
ISBN-13: 978-0-7459-5288-8

First edition 2007
10 9 8 7 6 5 4 3 2 1 0

A catalogue record for this book
is available from the British Library

The text paper used in this book has been
made from wood independently certified
as having come from sustainable forests.

Typeset in 10/12 Myriad Roman
Printed and bound in Malta
by Gutenberg Press

Contents

Introduction

The Bible is a very important book. I suppose nobody disputes that. It has shaped the civilization of the Western world, permeated much of its literature and been the inspiration of many of its greatest men and women. It still sells in a vast range of versions in over four thousand different languages. Yet to many people in the 'advanced' countries today it's unknown territory, partly, at least, because it does not immediately strike modern readers as talking about the world they live in.

All the same, many people would like to know what lies within those slightly daunting traditional covers. What sort of a book is this, that has exerted such a profound influence on our own civilization? What is its 'secret'? Is it really the word of God, a message from beyond to a human race trapped in time and space? Has it still got something to say that's as relevant to modern people in their technology as it obviously was to our ancestors in their tents?

Here the reader is offered a truly 'espresso' Bible – the power and impact of a shot of caffeine undiluted by too much milk and water! This is 'the Bible in sips', the heart of its story or message offered to the reader in carefully chosen extracts. The Bible has a 'plot', and each reading in this book falls somewhere in its unfolding story. It begins with tragedy – the human race (represented by one man and one woman) deciding that it knows better than its Creator, with dire consequences. It tells how the slow journey to restoration develops: the calling of one people (the descendants of Abraham) to be the means of blessing for the whole world; the giving to them of the Law, which sets out the principles of the good life; the words of their prophets, pointing to a time when a great rescuer or 'saviour' would be sent by God; and the coming of that saviour, Jesus, and the story of his life, death and resurrection from the dead. The last part of the story shows his followers on their new journey as pilgrims, living lives that will lead them to heaven.

I suppose the ideal consequence of reading this little book would be the customer hurrying off to buy the whole Bible and then reading it from cover to cover. If they did, they would find that the people it portrays and the things they say and do and care about are uncannily like ourselves and the things we say, do and care about in the very different world of the twenty-first century. Indeed, I hope this short selection will at least demonstrate that the Bible, while undoubtedly old, is not feeble and toothless. It can still administer a few shocks.

So, welcome to *The Espresso Bible!*

The Old Testament

Genesis

We start, of course, with the first book of the Bible, Genesis – the title simply means 'Beginning'. And Genesis in turn starts with the beginning of everything, the Bible's account of the creation. There were many such creation stories in the ancient world, but anyone reading them would have to acknowledge that the biblical story, cast as a kind of extended poem, is incomparably superior in almost every way. It has a clear theme – that everything that exists owes its origin to the mind and purpose of God. The process was orderly, moving from the universe itself to the appearance on earth of light, water, land and then, in order, vegetation, fish, birds, animals and finally, as the crown of it all, human beings, made 'in the image of God'.

The creation story is told twice, once from a cosmic viewpoint, and then from a human one, as we move into the beautiful 'Garden of Delights', Eden. There, in a story designed to show how the two sexes are complementary, the woman is created to join the man – and then, in a very different story, with tragic and long-term consequences, they decide together that they know better than God, disobey his instructions and are ejected from the Garden.

This is the Bible's explanation of the existence of evil in a world created by a good God. It is told in the form of a story, but its profound truth is that people cannot live the good life if they disregard the Maker's instructions!

Genesis 1:1–2:3

The Story of Creation
In the beginning God created the heavens and the earth. The earth was barren, with no form of life; it was under a roaring ocean covered with darkness. But the Spirit of God was moving over the water.

The First Day
God said, 'I command light to shine!' And light started shining. God looked at the light

and saw that it was good. He separated light
from darkness and named the light 'Day' and
the darkness 'Night'. Evening came and then
morning – that was the first day.

The Second Day
God said, 'I command a dome to separate the
water above it from the water below it.' And
that's what happened. God made the dome
and named it 'Sky'. Evening came and then
morning – that was the second day.

The Third Day
God said, 'I command the water under the
sky to come together in one place, so there
will be dry ground.' And that's what
happened. God named the dry ground
'Land', and he named the water 'Ocean'.
God looked at what he had done and saw that
it was good.

God said, 'I command the earth to
produce all kinds of plants, including fruit
trees and grain.' And that's what happened.
The earth produced all kinds of vegetation.
God looked at what he had done, and it was
good. Evening came and then morning – that
was the third day.

The Fourth Day
God said, 'I command lights to appear in the
sky and to separate day from night and to
show the time for seasons, special days and
years. I command them to shine on the earth.'
And that's what happened. God made two

powerful lights, the brighter one to rule the day and the other to rule the night. He also made the stars. Then God put these lights in the sky to shine on the earth, to rule day and night, and to separate light from darkness. God looked at what he had done, and it was good. Evening came and then morning – that was the fourth day.

The Fifth Day

God said, 'I command the ocean to be full of living creatures, and I command birds to fly above the earth.' So God made the giant sea monsters and all the living creatures that swim in the ocean. He also made every kind of bird. God looked at what he had done, and it was good. Then he gave the living creatures his blessing – he told the ocean creatures to live everywhere in the ocean and the birds to live everywhere on earth. Evening came and then morning – that was the fifth day.

The Sixth Day

God said, 'I command the earth to give life to all kinds of tame animals, wild animals and reptiles.' And that's what happened. God made every one of them. Then he looked at what he had done, and it was good.

God said, 'Now we will make humans, and they will be like us. We will let them rule the fish, the birds and all other living creatures.'

So God created humans to be like himself; he made men and women. God gave them his blessing and said: 'Have a lot of children! Fill the earth with people and bring it under your control. Rule over the fish in the ocean, the birds in the sky and every animal on the earth.

'I have provided all kinds of fruit and grain for you to eat. And I have given the green plants as food for everything else that breathes. These will be food for animals, both wild and tame, and for birds.'

God looked at what he had done. All of it was very good! Evening came and then morning – that was the sixth day.

So the heavens and the earth and everything else were created. By the seventh day God had finished his work, and so he rested. God blessed the seventh day and made it special because on that day he rested from his work.

Genesis 2:4–25

The Garden of Eden

When the Lord God made the heavens and the earth, no grass or plants were growing anywhere. God had not yet sent any rain, and there was no one to work the land. But streams came up from the ground and watered the earth. The Lord God took a handful of soil and made a man. God breathed life into the man, and the man started breathing. The Lord made a garden in a place called Eden, which was in the east, and he put the man there. The Lord God placed all kinds of beautiful trees and fruit trees in the garden. Two other trees were in the middle of the garden. One of the trees gave life – the other gave the power to know the difference between right and wrong...

The Lord God put the man in the Garden of Eden to take care of it and to look after it. But the Lord told him, 'You may eat fruit from any tree in the garden, except the one that has the power to let you know the difference between right and wrong. If you eat any fruit from that tree, you will die before the day is over!'

The Lord God said, 'It isn't good for the man to live alone. I need to make a suitable partner for him.' So the Lord took some soil and made animals and birds. He brought them to the man to see what names he would give each of them. Then the man named the tame animals and the birds and the wild animals. That's how they got their names.

None of these was the right kind of partner for the man. So the Lord God made him fall into a deep sleep, and he took out one of the man's ribs. Then, after closing the man's side, the Lord made a woman out of the rib.

The Lord God brought her to the man, and the man exclaimed, 'Here is someone like me! She is part of my body, my own flesh and bones. She came from me, a man. So I will name her Woman!' That's why a man will leave his own father and mother. He marries a woman, and the two of them become like one person.

Although the man and his wife were both naked, they were not ashamed.

Genesis 3

The First Sin

The snake was sneakier than any of the other wild animals that the Lord God had made. One day it came to the woman and asked, 'Did God tell you not to eat fruit from any tree in the garden?'

The woman answered, 'God said we could eat fruit from any tree in the garden, except the one in the middle. He told us not to eat fruit from that tree or even to touch it. If we do, we will die.'

'No, you won't!' the snake replied. 'God understands what will happen on the day you eat fruit from that tree. You will see what you have done, and you will know the difference between right and wrong, just as God does.'

The woman stared at the fruit. It looked beautiful and tasty. She wanted the wisdom that it would give her, and she ate some of the fruit. Her husband was there with her, so she gave some to him, and he ate it too. Right away they saw what they had done, and they realized they were naked. Then they sewed fig leaves together to make something to cover themselves.

Late in the afternoon a breeze began to blow, and the man and woman heard the Lord God walking in the garden. They were frightened and hid behind some trees.

The Trouble with Sin

The Lord called out to the man and asked, 'Where are you?'

The man answered, 'I was naked, and when I heard you walking through the garden, I was frightened and hid!'

'How did you know you were naked?' God asked. 'Did you eat any fruit from that tree in the middle of the garden?'

'It was the woman you put here with me,' the man said. 'She gave me some of the fruit, and I ate it.'

The Lord God then asked the woman, 'What have you done?'

'The snake tricked me,' she answered. 'And I ate some of that fruit.'

So the Lord God said to the snake: 'Because of what you have done, you will be the only animal to suffer this curse – for as long as you live, you will crawl on your stomach and eat dirt. You and this woman will hate each other; your descendants and hers will always be enemies. One of hers will strike you on the head, and you will strike him on the heel.'

Then the Lord said to the woman, 'You will suffer terribly when you give birth. But you will still desire your husband, and he will rule over you.'

The Lord said to the man, 'You listened to

your wife and ate fruit from that tree. And so, the ground will be under a curse because of what you did. As long as you live, you will have to struggle to grow enough food. Your food will be plants, but the ground will produce thorns and thistles. You will have to sweat to earn a living; you were made out of soil, and you will once again turn into soil.'

The man Adam named his wife Eve* because she would become the mother of all who live. Then the Lord God made clothes out of animal skins for the man and his wife. The Lord said, 'These people now know the difference between right and wrong, just as we do. But they must not be allowed to eat fruit from the tree that lets them live forever.' So the Lord God sent them out of the Garden of Eden, where they would have to work the ground from which the man had been made. Then God put winged creatures at the entrance to the garden and a flaming, flashing sword to guard the way to the life-giving tree.

[*Eve resembles the Hebrew word for 'living'.]

The Consequences of Sin
The disobedience of Adam and Eve is known as 'the Fall', because they had fallen from the beautiful innocence of the life they had enjoyed in Eden. The following part of Genesis begins to unfold some of the consequences of the Fall – the first murder (by Cain of his brother Abel) and then some

nameless wickedness involving the 'sons of God' taking wives from 'the children of men'. Anyway, God decided that the time had come to wipe out all this evil and start again – but to save one family, Noah's, in order to provide the basis for a new human race, together with representative animals to re-stock the earth. This, then, is the story of the Flood, Noah's Flood, as it is known – though in truth it was God's Flood.

Genesis 6:5–22

Noah's Ark

The Lord saw how bad the people on earth were and that everything they thought and planned was evil. He was very sorry that he had made them, and he said, 'I'll destroy every living creature on earth! I'll wipe out people, animals, birds and reptiles. I'm sorry I ever made them.'

But the Lord was pleased with Noah, and this is the story about him. Noah was the only person who lived right and obeyed God. He had three sons: Shem, Ham and Japheth.

God knew that everyone was terribly cruel and violent. So he told Noah: 'Cruelty and violence have spread everywhere. Now I'm going to destroy the whole earth and all its people. Get some good lumber and build a boat. Put rooms in it and cover it with tar inside and out. Make it four hundred and fifty feet long, seventy-five feet wide and forty-five feet high. Build a roof on the boat and leave a space of about eighteen inches between the roof and the sides. Make the boat three stories high and put a door on one side. I'm going to send a flood that will destroy everything that breathes! Nothing will be left alive. But I solemnly promise that you, your wife, your sons and your daughters-in-law will be kept safe in the boat. Bring into the boat with you a male and a female of every kind of animal and bird, as well as a male and a female of every reptile. I don't want them to be destroyed. Store up enough food both for yourself and for them.'

Noah did everything the Lord told him to do.

Genesis 7:1–24

The Flood

The Lord told Noah: 'Take your whole family with you into the boat, because you are the only one on this earth who pleases me. Take seven pairs of every kind of animal that can be used for sacrifice and one pair of all others. Also take seven pairs of every kind of bird with you. Do this so there will always be animals and birds on the earth. Seven days from now I will send rain that will last for forty days and nights, and I will destroy all other living creatures I have made.'

Noah was six hundred years old when he went into the boat to escape the flood, and he did everything the Lord had told him to do.

His wife, his sons and his daughters-in-law all went inside with him. He obeyed God and took a male and a female of each kind of animal and bird into the boat with him. Seven days later, a flood began to cover the earth.

Noah was six hundred years old when the water under the earth started gushing out everywhere. The sky opened like windows, and rain poured down for forty days and nights. All this began on the seventeenth day of the second month of the year. On that day Noah and his wife went into the boat with their three sons, Shem, Ham and Japheth, and their wives. They took along every kind of animal, tame and wild, including the birds. Noah took a male and a female of every living creature with him, just as God had told him to do. And when they were all in the boat, God closed the door.

For forty days the rain poured down without stopping. The water became deeper and deeper, until the boat started floating high above the ground. Finally, the mighty flood was so deep that even the highest mountain peaks were almost twenty-five feet below the surface of the water. Not a bird, animal, reptile or human was left alive anywhere on earth. The Lord destroyed everything that breathed. Nothing was left alive except Noah and the others in the boat.

A hundred and fifty days later, the water started going down.

Genesis 8:1–19

The Water Goes Down

God did not forget about Noah and the animals with him in the boat. So God made a wind blow, and the water started going down. God stopped up the places where the water had been gushing out from under the earth. He also closed up the sky, and the rain stopped. For a hundred and fifty days the water slowly went down. Then, on the seventeenth day of the seventh month of the year, the boat came to rest somewhere in the Ararat mountains. The water kept going down, and the mountain tops could be seen on the first day of the tenth month.

Forty days later Noah opened a window to send out a raven, but it kept flying around until the water had dried up. Noah wanted to find out if the water had gone down, and he sent out a dove. Deep water was still everywhere, and the dove could not find a place to land. So it flew back to the boat. Noah held out his hand and helped it back in.

Seven days later Noah sent the dove out again. It returned in the evening, holding in its beak a green leaf from an olive tree. Noah knew that the water was finally going down. He waited seven more days before sending the dove out again, and this time it did not return.

Noah was now six hundred and one years old. And by the first day of that year, almost all the water had gone away. Noah made an opening in the roof of the boat and saw that the ground was getting dry. By the twenty-seventh day of the second month, the earth was completely dry. God said to Noah, 'You, your wife, your sons and your daughters-in-law may now leave the boat. Let out the birds, animals and reptiles, so they can mate and live all over the earth.' After Noah and his family had gone out of the boat, the living creatures left in groups of their own kind.

Genesis 8:20–22

The Lord's Promise for the Earth

Noah built an altar where he could offer sacrifices to the Lord. Then he offered on the altar one of each kind of animal and bird that could be used for a sacrifice. The smell of the burnt offering pleased God, and he said: 'Never again will I punish the earth for the sinful things its people do. All of them have evil thoughts from the time they are young, but I will never destroy everything that breathes, as I did this time. As long as the earth remains, there will be planting and harvest, cold and heat; winter and summer, day and night.'

Abraham

The next great Bible event is undoubtedly the decision of a desert chieftain originally called Abram to leave his home in Ur, an ancient city of Chaldea, and travel westwards. He did this at what he took to be the prompting of a God he barely knew, but the prompting was so strong that he obeyed – with consequences which have shaped the religious history of the human race. From that one decision three great world religions were born – Judaism, the religion of the Jews, the descendants of Abram; Christianity, built on faith in Jesus of Nazareth, another descendant of Abram and, as its followers believe, the 'seed' promised to him; and Islam, which also takes Abram as its starting point of faith.

Abram travelled west, and had an encounter with God that changed his life. Subsequently his name was changed to 'Abraham', and the promise was given to him that through his 'seed' – his descendants – all the nations of the earth would one day be blessed. Our reading tells the story of his first call and his first encounter with the living God.

Genesis 12:1–7

The Lord Chooses Abram

The Lord said to Abram: 'Leave your country, your family and your relatives, and go to the land that I will show you. I will bless you and make your descendants into a great nation. You will become famous and be a blessing to others. I will bless anyone who blesses you, but I will put a curse on anyone who puts a curse on you. Everyone on earth will be blessed because of you.' Abram was seventy-five years old when the Lord told him to leave the city of Haran. He obeyed and left with his wife Sarai, his nephew Lot, and all the possessions and slaves they had gathered while in Haran.

When they came to the land of Canaan, Abram went as far as the sacred tree of Moreh in a place called Shechem. The Canaanites were still living in the land at that time, but the Lord appeared to Abram and promised, 'I will give this land to your family forever.' Abram then built an altar there for the Lord.

Exodus

This is the book of the great escape, an event still commemorated year after year by Jews in their Passover. Long after the days of

Abraham, his descendants ended up as slaves in Egypt. Joseph (he of the amazing technicolour dreamcoat!) had gone there as a slave, but ended up second only to Pharaoh. But after his death his contribution was forgotten, and his tribe, now settled in Egypt, was enslaved, set to build treasure houses under cruel taskmasters. Moses – through various adventures – had been brought up in the royal household, although he had been taught to believe in the God of his Hebrew ancestors. Now, however, he had fled to the desert region of Midian, where he had become a member of the family of a Midianite priest, Jethro. He was out on the hills with Jethro's sheep one day when the following event happened.

Exodus 3:1–10

God Speaks to Moses

One day, Moses was taking care of the sheep and goats of his father-in-law, Jethro, the priest of Midian, and Moses decided to lead them across the desert to Sinai, the holy mountain. There an angel of the Lord appeared to him from a burning bush. Moses saw that the bush was on fire, but it was not burning up. 'This is strange!' he said to himself. 'I'll go over and see why the bush isn't burning up.' When the Lord saw Moses coming near the bush, he called him by name, and Moses answered, 'Here I am.'

God replied, 'Don't come any closer. Take off your sandals – the ground where you are standing is holy. I am the God who was worshipped by your ancestors Abraham, Isaac and Jacob.'

Moses was afraid to look at God, and so he hid his face.

The Lord said: 'I have seen how my people are suffering as slaves in Egypt, and I have heard them beg for my help because of the way they are being mistreated. I feel sorry for them, and I have come down to rescue them from the Egyptians.

'I will bring my people out of Egypt into a country where there is good land, rich with milk and honey. I will give them the land where the Canaanites, Hittites, Amorites, Perizzites, Hivites and Jebusites now live. My people have begged for my help, and I have seen how cruel the Egyptians are to them. Now, go to the king! I am sending you to lead my people out of his country.'

The Flight from Egypt
Moses, albeit reluctantly, did what God commanded him, and returned to Egypt with his brother, Aaron. Powerfully backed up by the ten plagues sent by God upon Egypt, they finally persuaded Pharaoh to let the Hebrews (the 'Israelites') leave their country. On their last, fateful evening in Egypt – the night of the final, deadly plague

which killed all the firstborn sons of the Egyptians – the Israelites shared the 'Passover meal' which would guarantee their safety through the sacrifice of a lamb, whose blood was to be daubed on their doorposts. Then they left, a huge crowd heading westwards towards the Red Sea, led by Moses – swiftly to be followed by the chariots of Egypt, sent by Pharaoh, who had yet again changed his mind and intended to bring his slaves back to Egypt.

When the Israelites reached the water, they stopped – and became aware that in the distance were the chariots of Egypt, bearing down on them. They cried out to Moses, and he cried out to God.

Exodus 14:15–31

Crossing the Red Sea

The Lord said to Moses, 'Why do you keep calling out to me for help? Tell the Israelites to move forward. Then hold your walking stick over the sea. The water will open up and make a road where they can walk through on dry ground. I will make the Egyptians so stubborn that they will go after you. Then I will be praised because of what happens to the king and his chariots and cavalry. The Egyptians will know for sure that I am the Lord.'

All this time God's angel had gone ahead of Israel's army, but now he moved behind them. A large cloud had also gone ahead of them, but now it moved between the Egyptians and the Israelites. The cloud gave light to the Israelites, but made it dark for the Egyptians, and during the night they could not come any closer.

Moses stretched his arm over the sea, and the Lord sent a strong east wind that blew all night until there was dry land where the water had been. The sea opened up, and the Israelites walked through on dry land with a wall of water on each side.

The Egyptian chariots and cavalry went after them. But before daylight the Lord looked down at the Egyptian army from the fiery cloud and made them panic. Their chariot wheels got stuck, and it was hard for them to move. So the Egyptians said to one another, 'Let's leave these people alone! The Lord is on their side and is fighting against us.' The Lord told Moses, 'Stretch your arm towards the sea – the water will cover the Egyptians and their cavalry and chariots.' Moses stretched out his arm, and at daybreak the water rushed towards the Egyptians. They tried to run away, but the Lord drowned them in the sea. The water came and covered the chariots, the cavalry and the whole Egyptian army that had followed the Israelites into the sea. Not one of them was left alive. But the sea had made a wall of water on each side of the Israelites; so they walked through on dry land.

On that day, when the Israelites saw the bodies of the Egyptians washed up on the shore, they knew that the Lord had saved them. Because of the mighty power he had used against the Egyptians, the Israelites worshipped him and trusted him and his servant Moses.

Food in the Desert

As the Israelites – led by Moses, a man whose courage and leadership were outstanding, yet who several times made serious errors of judgment – set out across the several hundred miles of desert that lay between them and their 'Promised Land', they must have realized that both water and food would be recurring problems. Several times God led them to various sources of water at springs in the desert, but the food was provided in a more 'miraculous' way in the form of 'manna'. The people had complained to Moses that he had led them into the wilderness simply to let them die there of famine. He in turn sought God's help – and the Lord told him that he would 'rain down' food from heaven for the people! Here is what happened that night and the next morning.

Exodus 16:13–18

Manna – and More!

That evening a lot of quails came and landed everywhere in the camp, and the next morning dew covered the ground. After the dew had gone, the desert was covered with thin flakes that looked like frost. The people had never seen anything like this, and they started asking each other, 'What is it?'* Moses answered, 'This is the bread that the Lord has given you to eat. And he orders you to gather about two litres for each person in your family – that should be more than enough.'

They did as they were told. Some gathered more and some gathered less, according to their needs, and none was left over.

[* *Man-hu* in Hebrew means 'What is it?', hence the name 'manna'!]

Sinai

Eventually the Israelites reached Mount Sinai. Here Moses was commanded by God to climb the mountain to meet with him, and it was there, on the mountain top, that Moses was given the sacred Ten Commandments, the heart of the moral and ethical Law of Israel – and indeed of many subsequent civilizations, including those of Christendom. The whole event was surrounded by mystery and awe – thunder and lightning and even an earthquake, so that the people waiting nervously at the foot of the mountain wondered what was going on. In fact, while Moses was up the mountain (a long while, the proverbial 'forty days') they eventually came to the conclusion that he wasn't coming back, and persuaded Aaron to let them make a golden calf to worship – a direct contravention, of course, of the second of the Commandments.

Both these events – the giving of the Law and the disobedience of the people – had long-term consequences for the history of Israel.

Exodus 20:1–21

The Ten Commandments

God said to the people of Israel: 'I am the Lord your God, the one who brought you out of Egypt where you were slaves.

'Do not worship any god except me.

'Do not make idols that look like anything in the sky or on earth or in the ocean under the earth. Don't bow down and worship idols. I am the Lord your God, and I demand all your love. If you reject me, I will punish your families for three or four generations. But if you love me and obey my laws, I will be kind to your families for thousands of generations.

'Do not misuse my name. I am the Lord your God, and I will punish anyone who misuses my name.

'Remember that the Sabbath day belongs to me. You have six days when you can do your work, but the seventh day of each week belongs to me, your God. No one is to work on that day – not you, your children, your slaves, your animals or the foreigners who live in your towns. In six days I made the sky, the earth, the oceans, and everything in them, but on the seventh day I rested. That's why I made the Sabbath a special day that belongs to me.

'Respect your father and your mother, and you will live a long time in the land I am giving you.

'Do not murder.

'Be faithful in marriage.

'Do not steal.

'Do not tell lies about others.

'Do not desire anything that belongs to someone else. Don't desire anyone's house, wife or husband, slaves, oxen, donkeys or anything else.'

The People Are Afraid

The people trembled with fear when they heard the thunder and the trumpet and saw the lightning and the smoke coming from the mountain. They stood a long way off and said to Moses, 'If you speak to us, we will listen. But don't let God speak to us, or we will die!'

'Don't be afraid!' Moses replied. 'God has come only to test you, so that by obeying him you won't sin.' But when Moses went near the thick cloud where God was, the people stayed a long way off.

Deuteronomy

The Last Words of Moses

Moses is indisputably one of the greatest characters of the Bible and his influence on the history of the Jewish nation and of its religion was immense. These passages encapsulate his final words to the people, and were probably included by subsequent editors and compilers because they would serve as a constant warning of the dangers of religious compromise for a people surrounded by pagan nations, most of them worshipping an array of idols and indulging in such practices as human sacrifice. There is a reminder here, too, of the brutality that accompanied the conquest of Canaan. However, the chief concern of Moses was that the Law given at Sinai should be enshrined not only in the ark of the covenant ('the chest') but also in the hearts of the people.

Moses was succeeded by his 'lieutenant', Joshua – the name means 'saviour' – who would lead the people across the River Jordan and into the Promised Land.

Deuteronomy 31:1–12

Be Brave and Strong!

Moses again spoke to the whole nation of Israel: 'I am a hundred and twenty years old, and I am no longer able to be your leader. And besides that, the Lord your God has told me that he won't let me cross the Jordan River. But he has promised that he and Joshua will lead you across the Jordan to attack the nations that live on the other side. The Lord will destroy those nations just as he destroyed Sihon and Og, those two Amorite kings. Just remember – whenever you capture a place, kill everyone who lives there.

'Be brave and strong! Don't be afraid of the nations on the other side of the Jordan. The Lord your God will always be at your side, and he will never abandon you.'

Then Moses called Joshua up in front of the crowd and said: 'Joshua, be brave and strong as you lead these people into their land. The Lord made a promise long ago to Israel's ancestors that this land would someday belong to Israel. That time has now come, and you must divide up the land among the people. The Lord will lead you into the land. He will always be with you and help you, so don't ever be afraid of your enemies.'

Moses wrote down all of these laws and teachings and gave them to the priests and the leaders of Israel... And each new generation would listen and learn to worship the Lord their God with fear and trembling and to do exactly what is said in God's Law.

Deuteronomy 31:14–15, 23–28

Joshua is Appointed Leader

The Lord told Moses, 'You will soon die, so bring Joshua to the sacred tent, and I will appoint him the leader of Israel.'

Moses and Joshua went to the sacred tent, and the Lord appeared in a thick cloud right over the entrance to the tent...The Lord told Joshua, 'Be brave and strong! I will help you lead the people of Israel into the land that I have promised them.'

Moses wrote down all these laws and teachings in a book, then he went to the Levites who carried the sacred chest (the ark of the covenant) and said: 'This is the book of God's Law. Keep it beside the sacred chest that holds the agreement the Lord your God made with Israel. This book is proof that you know what the Lord wants you to do. I know how stubborn and rebellious you and the rest of the Israelites are. You have rebelled against the Lord while I have been alive, and it will only get worse after I am gone. So call together the leaders and officials of the tribes of Israel. I will bring this book and read every word of it to you, and I will call the sky and the earth as witnesses that all of you know what you are supposed to do.'

Joshua

Joshua duly led the Israelites to the edge of the Jordan River, ready to cross over into Canaan. It was spring, and the river was in spate, yet once the priests carrying the ark of the covenant ('the sacred chest') had entered the water, the river dried up and all the people were able to cross. This, then, was the second 'dry land' crossing of their long journey – with the ark of the Lord as the 'bridge'.

Joshua 3:1–17

Israel Crosses the Jordan River

Early the next morning, Joshua and the Israelites packed up and left Acacia. They went to the Jordan River and camped there that night. Two days later, their leaders went through the camp, shouting, 'When you see some of the priests carrying the sacred chest, you'll know it is time to cross to the other side. You've never been there before, and you won't know the way, unless you follow the chest. But don't get too close! Stay about half a mile back.'

Joshua told the people, 'Make yourselves acceptable to worship the Lord, because he is going to do some amazing things for us.'

Then Joshua turned to the priests and said, 'Take the chest and cross the Jordan River ahead of us.' So the priests picked up the chest by its carrying poles and went on ahead.

The Lord told Joshua, 'Beginning today, I will show the people that you are their leader, and they will know that I am helping you as I helped Moses. Now, tell the priests who are carrying the chest to go a little way into the river and stand there.'

Joshua spoke to the people: 'Come here and listen to what the Lord our God said he will do! The Canaanites, the Hittites, the Hivites, the Perizzites, the Girgashites, the Amorites and the Jebusites control the land on the other side of the river. But the living God will be with you and will force them out of the land when you attack. And now, God is going to prove that he's powerful enough to force them out. Just watch the sacred chest that belongs to the Lord, the ruler of the whole earth. As soon as the priests carrying the chest step into the Jordan, the water will stop flowing and pile up as if someone had built a dam across the river.'

The Lord had also said that each of the twelve tribes should choose one man to represent it. The Israelites packed up and left camp. The priests carrying the chest walked in front, until they came to the Jordan River. The water in the river had risen over its banks, as it often does in springtime. But as soon as the feet of the priests touched the water, the river stopped flowing, and the water started piling up at the town of Adam near Zarethan. No water flowed towards the Dead Sea, and the priests stood in the middle of the dry riverbed near Jericho while everyone else crossed over.

1 Samuel

Although this book bears his name, it is really an account of what happened in Israel during the period when Samuel was the Lord's 'prophet' – his spiritual representative and spokesman. Chief among these events were the public demand for a monarchy, the disastrous reign of the first king, Saul, and the anointing by Samuel of his chosen successor, David – at the time, a young shepherd boy from Bethlehem. He leapt to fame, however, through one dramatic incident, when the Philistines' champion, Goliath, a massive man, taunted the army of Israel to find an opponent for him.

1 Samuel 17:17–51

David and Goliath
One day, Jesse told David, 'Hurry and take this sack of roasted grain and these ten loaves

of bread to your brothers at the army camp.
And here are ten large chunks of cheese to
take to their commanding officer. Find out
how your brothers are doing and bring back
something that shows that they're all right.
They're with Saul's army, fighting the
Philistines in Elah Valley.'

David obeyed his father. He got up early
the next morning and left someone else in
charge of the sheep; then he loaded the
supplies and started off. He reached the army
camp just as the soldiers were taking their
places and shouting the battle cry. The army
of Israel and the Philistine army stood there
facing each other.

David left his things with the man in
charge of supplies and ran up to the battle
line to ask his brothers if they were well.
While David was talking with them, Goliath
came out from the line of Philistines and
started boasting as usual... David asked
some soldiers standing nearby, 'What will a
man get for killing this Philistine and
stopping him from insulting our people?
Who does that worthless Philistine think he
is? He's making fun of the army of the
living God!'...

Some soldiers overheard David talking,
so they told Saul what David had said. Saul
sent for David, and David came. 'Your
Majesty,' he said, 'this Philistine shouldn't
turn us into cowards. I'll go out and fight
him myself!'

'You don't have a chance against him,'

Saul replied. 'You're only a boy, and he's been a soldier all his life.'

But David told him: 'Your Majesty, I take care of my father's sheep. And when one of them is dragged off by a lion or a bear, I go after it and beat the wild animal until it lets the sheep go. If the wild animal turns and attacks me, I grab it by the throat and kill it. Sir, I have killed lions and bears that way, and I can kill this worthless Philistine. He shouldn't have made fun of the army of the living God! The Lord has rescued me from the claws of lions and bears, and he will keep me safe from the hands of this Philistine.'

'All right,' Saul answered, 'go ahead and fight him. And I hope the Lord will help you.'

Saul had his own military clothes and armour put on David, and he gave David a bronze helmet to wear. David strapped on a sword and tried to walk around, but he was not used to wearing these things.

'I can't move with all this stuff on,' David said. 'I'm just not used to it.'

David took off the armour and picked up his shepherd's stick. He went out to a stream and picked up five smooth rocks and put them in his leather bag. Then with his sling in his hand, he went straight towards Goliath.

David Kills Goliath

Goliath came towards David, walking behind the soldier who was carrying the giant's shield. When Goliath saw that David was just a healthy, good-looking boy, he made fun of him. 'Do you think I'm a dog?' Goliath asked. 'Is that why you've come after me with a stick?' He cursed David in the name of the Philistine gods and shouted, 'Come on! When I'm finished with you, I'll feed you to the birds and wild animals!'

David answered: 'You've come out to fight me with a sword and a spear and a dagger. But I've come out to fight you in the name of the Lord All-Powerful. He is the God of Israel's army, and you have insulted him too! Today the Lord will help me defeat you. I'll knock you down and cut off your head, and I'll feed the bodies of the other Philistine soldiers to the birds and wild animals. Then the whole world will know that Israel has a real God. Everybody here will see that the Lord doesn't need swords or spears to save his people. The Lord always wins his battles, and he will help us defeat you.'

When Goliath started forward, David ran towards him. He put a rock in his sling and swung the sling around by its straps. When he let go of one strap, the rock flew out and hit Goliath on the forehead. It cracked his skull, and he fell face down on the ground. David defeated Goliath with a sling and a rock. He killed him without even using a sword… When the Philistines saw what had happened to their hero, they started running away.

1 Kings

When David died he was succeeded by his
son, Solomon (noted for his wisdom), but
after that the monarchy went through a
long period of decline. The country split into
two, north (Israel) and south (Judah). There
were some good kings, but more bad ones;
some good periods, but more bad ones
when the people neglected their religious
obligations and copied their pagan
neighbours. The great prophets of Israel, of
whom Elijah was the first and greatest,
found themselves frequently in opposition
to the rulers. Elijah finally feared for his life
and fled, having incurred the wrath of the
notorious queen Jezebel. This story tells how
God met with him at the holy mountain of
Sinai.

1 Kings 19:8–13

The Lord Appears to Elijah

At last, he reached Mount Sinai, the
mountain of God, and he spent the night
there in a cave. While Elijah was on Mount
Sinai, the Lord asked, 'Elijah, why are you
here?'

He answered, 'Lord God All-Powerful, I've
always done my best to obey you. But your

people have broken their solemn promise to you. They have torn down your altars and killed all your prophets, except me. And now they are even trying to kill me!'

'Go out and stand on the mountain,' the Lord replied. 'I want you to see me when I pass by.'

All at once, a strong wind shook the mountain and shattered the rocks. But the Lord was not in the wind. Next, there was an earthquake, but the Lord was not in the earthquake. Then there was a fire, but the Lord was not in the fire.

Finally, there was a gentle breeze, and when Elijah heard it, he covered his face with his coat. He went out and stood at the entrance to the cave. The Lord asked: 'Elijah, why are you here?'

Job

The book starts with a story of disasters that befell Job – his whole family, his herds and flocks and houses were all lost. What follows is a lengthy dialogue between him and three 'comforters' on the huge question, 'Why do the innocent suffer?' The argument goes back and forth, until Job finally acknowledges that the answer lies beyond human understanding, and is

hidden in the deep wisdom of God. Our
passage is part of that moment of insight.

Job 42:1–6

Job's Reply to the Lord
Job said:

'No one can oppose you,
because you have the power to do what you
*   want.*
You asked why I talk so much when I know
*   so little.*
I have talked about things that are far beyond
*   my understanding.*

'You told me to listen
*   and answer your questions.*
I heard about you from others;
*   now I have seen you with my own eyes.*
That's why I hate myself
*   and sit here in dust and ashes*
*   to show my sorrow.'*

Psalms

The Psalms are the hymn book of Israel, written to be sung in worship. Traditionally many of them are ascribed to King David. They cover a vast range of emotions, needs and situations, but I have chosen three that seem to me to be splendid examples of Hebrew poetry and also demonstrate the breadth and insight of these remarkable writings.

Psalm 23

The 'Shepherd Psalm'

You, Lord, are my shepherd. I will never be in need.
You let me rest in fields of green grass.
You lead me to streams of peaceful water,
    and you refresh my life.
You are true to your name, and you lead me
    along the right paths.
I may walk through valleys as dark as death,
    but I won't be afraid.
You are with me,
    and your shepherd's rod makes me feel safe.
You treat me to a feast,
    while my enemies watch.

You honour me as your guest,
     and you fill my cup until it overflows.
Your kindness and love will always be with me
     each day of my life,
and I will live forever
     in your house, Lord.

Psalm 121

The Lord Will Protect His People

I look to the hills!
     Where will I find help?
It will come from the Lord,
     who created the heavens and the earth.
The Lord is your protector,
     and he won't go to sleep
     or let you stumble.
The protector of Israel doesn't doze
     or ever get drowsy.
The Lord is your protector,
     there at your right side
     to shade you from the sun.
You won't be harmed by the sun during the day
     or by the moon at night.
The Lord will protect you
     and keep you safe from all dangers.
The Lord will protect you,
     now and always,
     wherever you go.

Psalm 139:1–14

The Lord is Always Near

You have looked deep into my heart, Lord,
and you know all about me.
You know when I am resting or when I am
working,
and from heaven you discover my thoughts.
You notice everything I do
and everywhere I go.
Before I even speak a word,
you know what I will say,
and with your powerful arm
you protect me from every side.
I can't understand all of this!
Such wonderful knowledge is far above me.
Where could I go to escape
from your Spirit or from your sight?
If I were to climb up to the highest heavens,
you would be there.
If I were to dig down to the world of the dead
you would also be there.
Suppose I had wings like the dawning day
and flew across the ocean.
Even then your powerful arm would guide
and protect me.
Or suppose I said, 'I'll hide in the dark until
night comes to cover me over.'
But you see in the dark,
because daylight and dark
are all the same to you.
You are the one who put me together
inside my mother's body,

and I praise you because of the wonderful way
you created me.
Everything you do is marvellous!
Of this I have no doubt.

Ecclesiastes

The strange name means 'the preacher' and this is a book of wisdom – a bit world-weary at times! – by an anonymous writer. Both the passages I have chosen are well known, the first (on 'time') because it became the theme of a popular song in the sixties, and the second because it is such a vivid picture of the process of growing old!

Ecclesiastes 3:1–15

Everything Has Its Time

Everything on earth has its own time and its
own season.
There is a time for birth and death, planting
and reaping,
for killing and healing, destroying and
building,
for crying and laughing, weeping and
dancing,

for throwing stones and gathering stones,
  embracing and parting.
There is a time for finding and losing, keeping
  and giving,
for tearing and sewing, listening and speaking.
There is also a time for love and hate,
  for war and peace.

What do we gain by all of our hard work?
I have seen what difficult things God demands
of us. God makes everything happen at the
right time. Yet none of us can ever fully
understand all he has done, and he puts
questions in our minds about the past and the
future. I know the best thing we can do is
always to enjoy life, because God's gift to us is
the happiness we get from our food and drink
and from the work we do. Everything God has
done will last forever; nothing he does can
ever be changed. God has done all this, so that
we will worship him.

Everything that happens has happened before,
  and all that will be has already been –
  God does everything over and over again.

Ecclesiastes 12:1–7

Growing Old

Keep your Creator in mind while you are young!
In years to come, you will be burdened down with
  troubles and say, 'I don't enjoy life any more.'

Some day the light of the sun and the moon
and the stars will all seem dim to you.
Rain clouds will remain over your head.
Your body will grow feeble, your teeth will
decay and your eyesight fail.
The noisy grinding of grain will be shut out by
your deaf ears,
but even the song of a bird will keep you awake.
You will be afraid to climb up a hill or walk
down a road.
Your hair will turn as white as almond
blossoms.
You will feel lifeless and drag along like an
old grasshopper.
We each go to our eternal home, and the
streets are filled with those who mourn.
The silver cord snaps, the golden bowl breaks;
the water pitcher is smashed,
and the pulley at the well is shattered.
So our bodies return to the earth,
and the life-giving breath returns to God.

Song of Solomon

This is a book of love songs, a glorious
celebration of the wonder and beauty of
sexual love. Anyone who thinks the Bible is
'against' sex can't have read this book! Here
is one short taste of it.

Song of Solomon 2:10–14

He Speaks:

My darling, I love you!
Let's go away together.
Winter is past, the rain has stopped;
flowers cover the earth, it's time to sing.
The cooing of doves is heard in our land.
Fig trees are bearing fruit,
while blossoms on grapevines fill the air with
*   perfume.*
My darling, I love you!
Let's go away together.
You are my dove hiding among the rocks
*   on the side of a cliff.*
Let me see how lovely you are!
Let me hear the sound of your melodious
*   voice.*

Isaiah

The prophet Isaiah lived in the eighth
century BCE, when the dominant world
power was Assyria. He warned the kings
of Judah against the dangers of foreign
alliances and the dire consequences of
religious compromise. His warnings were
effective, but eventually a new power, the

Babylonians, conquered Judah in 587 BCE and took many of its people into captivity. The second half of the book (chapters 40 to 66) is a message of hope addressed to the people of that time. God had not forgotten them! Many of Isaiah's prophecies have been seen by Christians as relating to the coming Messiah, Jesus.

The first extract relates the call of Isaiah, on a momentous visit to the temple. The other four extracts contain words of hope, looking to the future time of blessing.

Isaiah 6:1–8

The Prophet's Call

In the year that King Uzziah died, I had a vision of the Lord. He was on his throne high above, and his robe filled the temple. Flaming creatures with six wings each were flying over him. They covered their faces with two of their wings and their bodies with two more. They used the other two wings for flying, as they shouted, 'Holy, holy, holy, Lord All-Powerful! The earth is filled with your glory.'

As they shouted, the doorposts of the temple shook, and the temple was filled with smoke. Then I cried out, 'I'm doomed! Everything I say is sinful, and so are the words of everyone around me. Yet I have seen the king, the Lord All-Powerful.'

One of the flaming creatures flew over to me with a burning coal that it had taken from the altar with a pair of metal tongs. It touched my lips with the hot coal and said, 'This has touched your lips. Your sins are forgiven, and you are no longer guilty.'

After this, I heard the Lord ask, 'Is there anyone I can send? Will someone go for us?'

'I'll go,' I answered. 'Send me!'

Isaiah 9:1–7

War is Over

Those who walked in the dark have seen a
*   bright light.*
And it shines upon everyone who lives in the
*   land of darkest shadows.*
Our Lord, you have made your nation
*   stronger.*
Because of you, its people are glad and
*   celebrate like workers at harvest time,*
or like soldiers dividing up what they have
*   taken.*
You have broken the power of those who
*   abused and enslaved your people.*
You have rescued them just as you saved your
*   people from Midian.*
The boots of marching warriors and the
*   bloodstained uniforms*
have been fed to flames and eaten by fire.

A Child Has Been Born

A child has been born for us.
We have been given a son who will be our
ruler.
His names will be Wonderful Advisor and
Mighty God,
Eternal Father and Prince of Peace.
His power will never end; peace will last
forever.
He will rule David's kingdom and make it
grow strong.
He will always rule with honesty and justice.
The Lord All-Powerful will make certain
that all of this is done.

Isaiah 11

Peace at Last

Like a branch that sprouts from a stump,
someone from David's family will some day
be king.
The Spirit of the Lord will be with him
to give him understanding, wisdom and
insight.
He will be powerful, and he will know
and honour the Lord.
His greatest joy will be to obey the Lord.
This king won't judge by appearances or listen
to rumours.
The poor and the needy will be treated with
fairness and with justice.

His word will be law everywhere in the land,
    and criminals will be put to death.
Honesty and fairness will be his royal robes.
Leopards will lie down with young goats,
    and wolves will rest with lambs.
Calves and lions will eat together
    and be cared for by little children.
Cows and bears will share the same pasture;
    their young will rest side by side.
Lions and oxen will both eat straw.
Little children will play near snake holes.
They will stick their hands into dens of
    poisonous snakes
and never be hurt.
Nothing harmful will take place on the Lord's
    holy mountain.
Just as water fills the sea,
the land will be filled with people who know
    and honour the Lord.

Isaiah 35:5–10

The Land and its People Transformed

The blind will see, and the ears of the deaf
    will be healed.
Those who were lame will leap around like
    deer;
tongues once silent will begin to shout.
Water will rush through the desert.
Scorching sand will turn into a lake,

and thirsty ground will flow with fountains.
Grass will grow in wetlands,
where packs of wild dogs once made their
   home.

God's Sacred Highway

A good road will be there, and it will be
   named
'God's Sacred Highway.'
It will be for God's people;
no one unfit to worship God
   will walk on that road,
and no fools can travel on that highway.
No lions or other wild animals will come near
   that road;
only those the Lord has saved will travel there.
The people the Lord has rescued will come
   back singing as they enter Zion.
Happiness will be a crown they will always
   wear.
They will celebrate and shout because all
   sorrows and worries
will be gone far away.

Isaiah 40:1-5

The Voice in the Wilderness

Our God has said: 'Encourage my people!
Give them comfort. Speak kindly to Jerusalem
   and announce: Your slavery is past;
   your punishment is over.

I, the Lord, made you pay
    double for your sins.'
Someone is shouting: 'Clear a path in the
    desert!
Make a straight road for the Lord our God.
Fill in the valleys; flatten every hill and
    mountain.
Level the rough and rugged ground.
Then the glory of the Lord will appear for all
    to see.
The Lord has promised this!'

Ezekiel

We have two extracts from the prophecies of Ezekiel, who lived in the sixth century BCE.

He warned the people of coming disaster, though like Isaiah and Jeremiah there is also always a note of hope that in the end God will vindicate and save his people. Here are two of his most powerful and memorable pieces of writing – first, an extraordinary vision of the glory of God, and then the well-known metaphor of the dry bones that come to life.

Ezekiel 1:4-28

A Vision of God's Glory

I saw a windstorm blowing in from the north.
Lightning flashed from a huge cloud and lit
up the whole sky with a dazzling brightness.
The fiery centre of the cloud was as shiny as
polished metal, and in that centre I saw what
looked like four living creatures. They were
somewhat like humans, except that each one
had four faces and four wings. Their legs were
straight, but their feet looked like the hoofs of
calves and sparkled like bronze. Under each
of their wings, these creatures had a human
hand. The four creatures were standing back
to back with the tips of their wings touching.
They moved together in every direction,
without turning their bodies.

Each creature had the face of a human in
front, the face of a lion on the right side, the
face of a bull on the left, and the face of an
eagle at the back. Two wings of each creature
were spread out and touched the wings of the
creatures on either side. The other two wings
of each creature were folded against its body.
Wherever the four living creatures went, they
moved together without turning their bodies,
because each creature faced straight ahead.
The creatures were glowing like hot coals, and
I saw something like a flaming torch moving
back and forth among them. Lightning
flashed from the torch every time its flame
blazed up. The creatures themselves moved as

quickly as sparks jumping from a fire. I then noticed that on the ground beside each of the four living creatures was a wheel, shining like chrysolite. Each wheel was exactly the same and had a second wheel that cut through the middle of it, so that they could move in any direction without turning. The rims of the wheels were large and had eyes all the way around them. The creatures controlled when and where the wheels moved – the wheels went wherever the four creatures went and stopped whenever they stopped. Even when the creatures flew in the air, the wheels were beside them. Above the living creatures, I saw something that was sparkling like ice, and it reminded me of a dome. Each creature had two of its wings stretched out towards the creatures on either side, with the other two wings folded against its body. Whenever the creatures flew, their wings roared like an ocean or a large army or even the voice of God All-Powerful. And whenever the creatures stopped, they folded their wings against their bodies.

When the creatures stopped flapping their wings, I heard a sound coming from above the dome. I then saw what looked like a throne made of sapphire, and sitting on the throne was a figure in the shape of a human. From the waist up, it was glowing like metal in a hot furnace, and from the waist down it looked like the flames of a fire. The figure was surrounded by a bright light, as colourful as a rainbow that appears after a storm. I realized I was seeing the brightness of the Lord's glory! So I bowed with my face to the ground, and just then I heard a voice speaking to me.

Ezekiel 37

Dry Bones Live Again

Some time later, I felt the Lord's power take control of me, and his Spirit carried me to a valley full of bones. The Lord showed me all around, and everywhere I looked I saw bones that were dried out. He said, 'Ezekiel, son of man, can these bones come back to life?'

I replied, 'Lord God, only you can answer that.'

He then told me to say: 'Dry bones, listen to what the Lord is saying to you, "I, the Lord God, will put breath in you, and once again you will live. I will wrap you with muscles and skin and breathe life into you. Then you will know that I am the Lord."'

I did what the Lord said, but before I finished speaking, I heard a rattling noise. The bones were coming together! I saw muscles and skin cover the bones, but they had no life in them.

The Lord said: 'Ezekiel, now say to the wind, "The Lord God commands you to blow from every direction and to breathe life into these dead bodies, so they can live again."' As soon as I said this, the wind blew among the bodies, and they came back to life! They all stood up, and there were enough to make a large army.

The Lord said: 'Ezekiel, the people of Israel are like dead bones. They complain that they are dried up and that they have no hope for the future. So tell them, "I, the Lord God, promise to open your graves and set you free. I will bring you back to Israel, and when that happens, you will realize that I am the Lord. My Spirit will give you breath, and you will live again. I will bring you home, and you will know that I have kept my promise. I, the Lord, have spoken."'

Jonah

Most people just think of 'Jonah in the whale's belly', but actually this short book is about repentance and doing God's will. Jonah was reluctant to go to preach to the people of the city of Nineveh (which led to all the incidents on his journey, including being swallowed by the big fish!), and when he got there he was angry that the people repented at his preaching, instead of facing the punishment he thought they deserved. In our passage, God teaches him a lesson about God's priorities.

Jonah 3:10–4:11

God's Concern for Nineveh

When God saw that the people had stopped
doing evil things, he had pity and did not
destroy them as he had planned. Jonah was
really upset and angry. So he prayed: 'Our
Lord, I knew from the very beginning that you
wouldn't destroy Nineveh. That's why I left my
own country and headed for Spain. You are
a kind and merciful God, and you are very
patient. You always show love, and you don't
like to punish anyone, not even foreigners. Now
let me die! I'd be better off dead.'

The Lord replied, 'What right do you have
to be angry?'

Jonah then left through the east gate of the
city and made a shelter to protect himself
from the sun. He sat under the shelter, waiting
to see what would happen to Nineveh.

The Lord made a vine grow up to shade
Jonah's head and protect him from the sun.
Jonah was very happy to have the vine, but
early the next morning the Lord sent a worm
to chew on the vine, and the vine dried up.
During the day the Lord sent a scorching
wind, and the sun beat down on Jonah's head,
making him feel faint. Jonah was ready to die,
and he shouted, 'I wish I were dead!'

But the Lord asked, 'Jonah, do you have
the right to be angry about the vine?'

'Yes, I do,' he answered, 'and I'm angry
enough to die.'

But the Lord said, 'You are concerned about a vine that you did not plant or take care of, a vine that grew up in one night and died the next. In that city of Nineveh there are more than a hundred and twenty thousand people who cannot tell right from wrong, and many cattle are also there. Don't you think I should be concerned about that big city?'

Daniel

Daniel was a Jew who had been taken into captivity in Babylon, where he continued to observe his daily devotions and prayers. These contradicted an edict of King Darius, and local leaders who disliked Daniel forced the king to apply his ruling to the young Jew – that he should be fed to the lions. Reluctantly, Darius felt he had to go ahead with it.

Daniel 6:16–23

Daniel in the Lions' Den

So King Darius ordered Daniel to be brought out and thrown into a pit of lions. But he said to Daniel, 'You have been faithful to your God, and I pray that he will rescue you.'

A stone was rolled over the pit, and it was sealed. Then Darius and his officials stamped the seal to show that no one should let Daniel out. All night long the king could not sleep. He did not eat anything, and he would not let anyone come in to entertain him.

At daybreak the king got up and ran to the pit. He was anxious and shouted, 'Daniel, you were faithful and served your God. Was he able to save you from the lions?'

Daniel answered, 'Your Majesty, I hope you live forever! My God knew that I was innocent, and he sent an angel to keep the lions from eating me. Your Majesty, I have never done anything to hurt you.'

The king was relieved to hear Daniel's voice, and he gave orders for him to be taken out of the pit. Daniel's faith in his God had kept him from being harmed.

Amos

Amos prophesied in the eighth century BCE. Like others he foretold disaster if the nation did not repent and return to God, but also like them, he drew pictures of times of future blessing if they turned back to the Lord. Here is one of them.

Amos 9:13–15

True Prosperity

You will have such a harvest
that you won't be able to bring in all of your
*   wheat before ploughing time.*
You will have grapes left over from season to
*   season;*
your fruitful vineyards will cover the
*   mountains.*
I'll make Israel prosper again.
*   You will rebuild your towns and live in them.*
You will drink wine from your own vineyards
*   and eat the fruit you grow.*
I'll plant your roots deep in the land I have
*   given you,*
and you won't ever be uprooted again.
I, the Lord God, have spoken!

Micah

Micah was a contemporary of Isaiah, and
his short book – one of the so-called Minor
Prophets – echoes many of the great
prophet's ideas. Like Isaiah, Micah is
concerned about religious compromise
and corruption, especially in high places.
Like Isaiah he warns of the dreadful
consequences of continued disobedience.

But also like Isaiah, and all the others, he offers an enthralling vision of hope and blessing if God's people return to his ways. Here we have three short extracts from his book. The first is a picture of a golden future of peace and prosperity, perhaps one of the most often quoted passages from Hebrew prophecy. The second is a prophecy relating to the little town of Bethlehem and a future 'ruler' of Israel – taken by Matthew in the New Testament as fulfilled in the coming of Jesus, born in that place. The third is a summary of the whole prophetic message – what is it God requires of us?

Micah 4:1–5

Peace and Prosperity

In the future, the mountain with the Lord's temple
will be the highest of all.
It will reach above the hills, and every nation will rush to it.
People of many nations will come and say,
'Let's go up to the mountain of the Lord God of Jacob
and worship in his temple.'
The Lord will teach us his Law from Jerusalem, and we will obey him.
He will settle arguments between distant and powerful nations.

They will pound their swords and their spears
    into rakes and shovels;
they will never again make war or attack one
    another.
Everyone will find rest beneath their own fig
    trees or grape vines,
and they will live in peace.
This is a solemn promise of the Lord All-
    Powerful.
Others may follow their gods, but we will
    always follow
the Lord our God.

Micah 5:2

A Promise for Bethlehem

Bethlehem Ephrath,
you are one of the smallest towns in the nation
    of Judah.
But the Lord will choose one of your people
    to rule the nation –
someone whose family goes back to ancient
    times.

Micah 6:6–8

True Obedience

What offering should I bring when I bow
    down to worship the Lord God Most High?

Should I try to please him by sacrificing calves
  a year old?
Will thousands of sheep or rivers of olive oil
  make God satisfied with me?
Should I sacrifice to the Lord my firstborn
  child
as payment for my terrible sins?
The Lord God has told us what is right and
  what he demands:
'See that justice is done, let mercy be your first
  concern,
and humbly obey your God.'

Malachi

Malachi – the name means 'my messenger' –
is the last voice of the Old Testament in the
Bible as Christians have it. He lived in the fifth
century BCE, before the long occupations by
Greeks and then Romans which led up to the
time of Jesus. He is particularly angry about
corruption in the Temple itself and among
the priests, as well as of the people's failure
to offer the due sacrifices and tithes.
Nevertheless, he promises that the 'Lord's
messenger' will come 'suddenly', but his
coming will bring judgment as well as
blessing. For those who honour God's name
there will be healing and joy. Here are two
short passages from this book.

Malachi 3:1–4

The Promised Messenger

I, the Lord All-Powerful, will send my messenger to prepare the way for me. Then suddenly the Lord you are looking for will appear in his temple. The messenger you desire is coming with my promise, and he is on his way.

On the day the Lord comes, he will be like a furnace that purifies silver or like strong soap in a washbasin. No one will be able to stand up to him. The Lord will purify the descendants of Levi,* as though they were gold or silver. Then they will bring the proper offerings to the Lord, and the offerings of the people of Judah and Jerusalem will please him, just as they did in the past.

[* The priestly tribe]

Malachi 4:1, 2, 4–6

The Day of Judgment

The Lord said: 'The day of judgment is certain to come. And it will be like a red-hot furnace with flames that burn up proud and sinful people, as though they were straw. Not a branch or a root will be left. I, the Lord All-Powerful, have spoken! But for you that honour my name, victory will shine like the sun with healing in its rays, and you will jump around like calves at play...

Don't ever forget the laws and teachings I gave my servant Moses on Mount Sinai. I, the Lord, promise to send the prophet Elijah before that great and terrible day comes. He will lead children and parents to love each other more, so that when I come, I won't bring doom to the land.'

The New Testament

The New Testament (the Christian
Scriptures) was written by a variety of
authors between about 65 CE and 100 CE.
The test of its authenticity was whether the
books had 'apostolic' authority – that's to
say, were they written either by the apostles
themselves (the eyewitnesses of the life and
resurrection of Jesus) or by people closely
associated with them. There are four
'Gospels', telling the story of the life,
teaching, death and rising of Jesus from
different perspectives; the book of Acts,
which tells the story of the first Christians
and the shaping of the church; letters from
prominent church leaders (Paul, Peter, James
and John among them) and finally the
vision, by a man called John, of heaven and
the final purposes of God.

Matthew

Matthew's Gospel is placed first, not
because it was the first to be written but
because it provides a clear link between
the Hebrew Scriptures (the Old Testament)
and the Christian Scriptures (the New
Testament). He is almost obsessively
concerned to demonstrate that everything
Jesus said and did was in fulfilment of the
Jewish prophets. Matthew also brings
together the teaching and parables
(teaching stories) of Jesus in an organized
way, including the great Sermon on the
Mount, from which we have several
extracts. We start, however, with the visit to
the infant Jesus of the mysterious 'wise
men' (*Magi*) from the east – representatives
of the old era of superstition and spells.
Significantly, they lay their gifts at the feet
of the infant Jesus.

Matthew 2:1–12

The Wise Men

When Jesus was born in the village of
Bethlehem in Judea, Herod was king. During
this time some wise men from the east came
to Jerusalem and said, 'Where is the child

born to be king of the Jews? We saw his star in the east and have come to worship him.' When King Herod heard about this, he was worried, and so was everyone else in Jerusalem. Herod brought together the chief priests and the teachers of the Law of Moses and asked them, 'Where will the Messiah be born?'

They told him, 'He will be born in Bethlehem, just as the prophet wrote: "Bethlehem in the land of Judea, you are very important among the towns of Judea. From your town will come a leader, who will be like a shepherd for my people, Israel."'

Herod secretly called in the wise men and asked them when they had first seen the star. He told them, 'Go to Bethlehem and search carefully for the child. As soon as you find him, let me know. I want to go and worship him too.'

The wise men listened to what the king said and then left. The star they had seen in the east went on ahead of them until it stopped over the place where the child was. They were thrilled and excited to see the star.

When the men went into the house and saw the child with Mary, his mother, they knelt down and worshipped him. They took out their gifts of gold, frankincense and myrrh and gave them to him. Later they were warned in a dream not to return to Herod, and they went back home by another road.

The Sermon on the Mount

This is a collection of the teachings of Jesus. If it has a central theme, it is 'priorities' – understanding what is truly important, and what is not. There are three extracts from it here. The first is the collection of sayings known as the Beatitudes – a list of the qualities that bring about God's blessing on us and so make us 'happy'. The second is the famous saying of Jesus about loving our enemies. The third is about the worries of everyday life. These are followed by three other extracts from the teaching of Jesus.

Matthew 5:1–12

The Beatitudes

When Jesus saw the crowds, he went up on the side of a mountain and sat down. Jesus' disciples gathered around him, and he taught them:

'God blesses those people who depend only on him. They belong to the kingdom of heaven!

'God blesses those people who grieve. They will find comfort!

'God blesses those people who are humble. The earth will belong to them!

'God blesses those people who want to obey him more than to eat or drink. They will be given what they want!

'God blesses those people who are merciful. They will be treated with mercy!

'God blesses those people whose hearts are pure. They will see him!

'God blesses those people who make peace. They will be called his children!

'God blesses those people who are treated badly for doing right. They belong to the kingdom of heaven.

'God will bless you when people insult you, mistreat you, and tell all kinds of evil lies about you because of me. Be happy and excited! You will have a great reward in heaven. People did these same things to the prophets who lived long ago.'

Matthew 5:38–48

Love

'You know that you have been taught, "An eye for an eye and a tooth for a tooth." But I tell you not to try to get even with a person who has done something to you. When someone slaps your right cheek, turn and let that person slap your other cheek. If someone sues you for your shirt, give up your coat as well. If a soldier forces you to carry his pack one mile, carry it two miles. When people ask you for something, give it to them. When they want to borrow money, lend it to them.

'You have heard people say, "Love your neighbours and hate your enemies." But I tell you to love your enemies and pray for anyone who mistreats you. Then you will be acting like your Father in heaven. He makes the sun rise on both good and bad people. And he sends rain for the ones who do right and for the ones who do wrong. If you love only those people who love you, will God reward you for that? Even tax collectors love their friends. If you greet only your friends, what's so great about that? Don't even unbelievers do that? But you must always act like your Father in heaven.'

Matthew 6:25–34

Don't Worry!

'I tell you not to worry about your life. Don't worry about having something to eat, drink or wear. Isn't life more than food or clothing? Look at the birds in the sky! They don't plant or harvest. They don't even store grain in barns. Yet your Father in heaven takes care of them. Aren't you worth more than birds?

'Can worry make you live longer? Why worry about clothes? Look how the wild flowers grow. They don't work hard to make their clothes. But I tell you that Solomon with all his wealth wasn't as well clothed as one of them. God gives such beauty to everything that grows in the fields, even though it is here today and thrown into a fire tomorrow. He will surely do even more for you! Why do you have such little faith? Don't worry and ask yourselves, "Will we have anything to eat? Will we have anything to drink? Will we have any clothes to wear?" Only people who don't know God are always worrying about such things. Your Father in heaven knows that you need all of these. But more than anything else, put God's work first and do what he wants. Then the other things will be yours as well.

'Don't worry about tomorrow. It will take care of itself. You have enough to worry about today.'

Matthew 11:25–30

An Invitation to the Weary

At that moment Jesus said: 'My Father, Lord of heaven and earth, I am grateful that you hid all this from wise and educated people and showed it to ordinary people. Yes, Father, that is what pleased you.

'My Father has given me everything, and he is the only one who knows the Son. The only one who truly knows the Father is the Son. But the Son wants to tell others about the Father, so that they can know him too.

'If you are tired from carrying heavy
burdens, come to me and I will give you rest
Take the yoke I give you. Put it on your
shoulders and learn from me. I am gentle and
humble, and you will find rest. This yoke is
easy to bear, and this burden is light.'

Matthew 13:44–46

A Hidden Treasure

'The kingdom of heaven is like what happens
when someone finds a treasure hidden in a
field and buries it again. A person like that is
happy and goes and sells everything in order
to buy that field.'

A Valuable Pearl

'The kingdom of heaven is like what happens
when a shop owner is looking for fine pearls.
After finding a very valuable one, the owner
goes and sells everything in order to buy that
pearl.'

Mark

This is the earliest, shortest and most
succinct of the Gospels, so I shall use it
to outline the story of the life of Jesus,

beginning not with his birth but with his 'forerunner', John the Baptist, and Jesus' own baptism. We continue with one of Jesus' healing miracles; the moment when the disciples openly confess that they believe him to be the 'Messiah', the Christ, whom God has sent; and the transfiguration, which confirmed that truth in their hearts. We go then to the last supper, the betrayal in the Garden of Gethsemane, the mock trial and the crucifixion. We end the extracts from this Gospel with Mark's very brief but convincing account of the morning of the resurrection.

Mark 1:1–15

The Preaching of John the Baptist

This is the good news about Jesus Christ, the Son of God. It began just as God had said in the book written by Isaiah the prophet, 'I am sending my messenger to get the way ready for you. In the desert someone is shouting, "Get the road ready for the Lord! Make a straight path for him."'

So John the Baptist showed up in the desert and told everyone, 'Turn back to God and be baptized! Then your sins will be forgiven.'

From all Judea and Jerusalem crowds of people went to John. They confessed how sorry they were for their sins, and he baptized them in the Jordan River.

John wore clothes made of camel's hair. He had a leather strap around his waist and ate grasshoppers and wild honey.

John also told the people, 'Someone more powerful is going to come. And I am not good enough even to stoop down and untie his sandals. I baptize you with water, but he will baptize you with the Holy Spirit!'

The Baptism of Jesus

About that time Jesus came from Nazareth in Galilee, and John baptized him in the Jordan River. As soon as Jesus came out of the water, he saw the sky open and the Holy Spirit coming down to him like a dove. A voice from heaven said, 'You are my own dear Son, and I am pleased with you.'

Jesus and Satan

Right away God's Spirit made Jesus go into the desert. He stayed there for forty days while Satan tested him. Jesus was with the wild animals, but angels took care of him.

Jesus Begins His Work

After John was arrested, Jesus went to Galilee and told the good news that comes from God. He said, 'The time has come! God's kingdom will soon be here. Turn back to God and believe the good news!'

Mark 2:1–12

Jesus Heals a Crippled Man

Jesus went back to Capernaum, and a few days later people heard that he was at home. Then so many of them came to the house that there wasn't even standing room left in front of the door.

Jesus was still teaching when four people came up, carrying a crippled man on a mat. But because of the crowd, they could not get him to Jesus. So they made a hole in the roof above him and let the man down in front of everyone.

When Jesus saw how much faith they had, he said to the crippled man, 'My friend, your sins are forgiven.'

Some of the teachers of the Law of Moses were sitting there. They started wondering, 'Why would he say such a thing? He must think he is God! Only God can forgive sins.'

Right away, Jesus knew what they were thinking, and he said, 'Why are you thinking such things? Is it easier for me to tell this crippled man that his sins are forgiven or to tell him to get up and pick up his mat and go on home? I will show you that the Son of Man has the right to forgive sins here on earth.' So Jesus said to the man, 'Get up! Pick up your mat and go on home.'

The man got right up. He picked up his mat and went out while everyone watched in amazement. They praised God and said, 'We have never seen anything like this!'

Mark 8:27–30

Who is Jesus?

Jesus and his disciples went to the villages near the town of Caesarea Philippi. As they were walking along, he asked them, 'What do people say about me?'

The disciples answered, 'Some say you are John the Baptist or maybe Elijah. Others say you are one of the prophets.'

Then Jesus asked them, 'But who do you say I am?'

'You are the Messiah!' Peter replied.

Jesus warned the disciples not to tell anyone about him.

Mark 9:2–10

The True Glory of Jesus

Six days later Jesus took Peter, James and John with him. They went up on a high mountain, where they could be alone. There in front of the disciples, Jesus was completely changed. His clothes became much whiter than any bleach on earth could make them. Then Moses and Elijah were there talking with Jesus.

Peter said to Jesus, 'Teacher, it is good for us to be here! Let us make three shelters, one for you, one for Moses, and one for Elijah.' But Peter and the others were terribly frightened, and he did not know what he was talking about.

The shadow of a cloud passed over and covered them. From the cloud a voice said, 'This is my Son, and I love him. Listen to what he says!' At once the disciples looked around, but they saw only Jesus.

As Jesus and his disciples were coming down the mountain, he told them not to say a word about what they had seen, until the Son of Man had been raised from death. So they kept it to themselves. But they wondered what he meant by the words 'raised from death'.

Mark 14:17–50

The Night of the Betrayal

While Jesus and the twelve disciples were eating together that evening, he said, 'The one who will betray me is now eating with me.'

This made the disciples sad, and one after another they said to Jesus, 'You surely don't mean me!'

He answered, 'It is one of you twelve men who are eating from this dish with me. The Son of Man will die, just as the Scriptures say.

But it is going to be terrible for the one who betrays me. That man would be better off if he had never been born.'

The Lord's Supper

During the meal Jesus took some bread in his hands. He blessed the bread and broke it. Then he gave it to his disciples and said, 'Take this. It is my body.'

Jesus picked up a cup of wine and gave thanks to God. He gave it to his disciples, and they all drank some. Then he said, 'This is my blood, which is poured out for many people, and with it God makes his agreement. From now on I will not drink any wine, until I drink new wine in God's kingdom.' Then they sang a hymn and went out to the Mount of Olives.

Peter's Promise

Jesus said to his disciples, 'All of you will reject me, as the Scriptures say, "I will strike down the shepherd, and the sheep will be scattered." But after I am raised to life, I will go ahead of you to Galilee.'

Peter spoke up. 'Even if all the others reject you, I never will!'

Jesus replied, 'This very night before a rooster crows twice, you will say three times that you don't know me.'

But Peter was so sure of himself that he said, 'Even if I have to die with you, I will never say that I don't know you!' All the others said the same thing.

Jesus Prays

Jesus went with his disciples to a place called Gethsemane, and he told them, 'Sit here while I pray.'

Jesus took along Peter, James and John. He was sad and troubled and told them, 'I am so sad that I feel as if I am dying. Stay here and keep awake with me.'

Jesus walked on a little way. Then he knelt down on the ground and prayed, 'Father, if it is possible, don't let this happen to me! Father, you can do anything. Don't make me suffer by having me drink from this cup. But do what you want, and not what I want.'

When Jesus came back and found the disciples sleeping, he said to Simon Peter, 'Are you asleep? Can't you stay awake for just one hour? Stay awake and pray that you won't be tested. You want to do what is right, but you are weak.'

Jesus went back and prayed the same prayer. But when he returned to the disciples, he found them sleeping again. They simply could not keep their eyes open, and they did not know what to say.

When Jesus returned to the disciples the third time, he said, 'Are you still sleeping and resting? Enough of that! The time has come for the Son of Man to be handed over to sinners. Get up! Let's go. The one who will betray me is already here.'

Jesus is Arrested

Jesus was still speaking when Judas the betrayer came up. He was one of the twelve disciples, and a mob of men armed with swords and clubs was with him. They had been sent by the chief priests, the nation's leaders, and the teachers of the Law of Moses. Judas had told them ahead of time, 'Arrest the man I greet with a kiss. Tie him up tight and lead him away.'

Judas walked right up to Jesus and said, 'Teacher!' Then Judas kissed him, and the men grabbed Jesus and arrested him.

Someone standing there pulled out a sword. He struck the servant of the high priest and cut off his ear.

Jesus said to the mob, 'Why do you come with swords and clubs to arrest me like a criminal? Day after day I was with you and taught in the temple, and you didn't arrest me. But what the Scriptures say must come true.'

All of Jesus' disciples ran off and left him.

Mark 15:25–39

The Crucifixion

It was about nine o'clock in the morning when they nailed Jesus to the cross. On it was a sign that told why he was nailed there. It read, 'This is the King of the Jews.' The soldiers also nailed two criminals on crosses, one to the right of Jesus and the other to his left.

People who passed by said terrible things about Jesus. They shook their heads and shouted, 'Ha! So you're the one who claimed you could tear down the temple and build it again in three days. Save yourself and come down from the cross!'

The chief priests and the teachers of the Law of Moses also made fun of Jesus. They said to each other, 'He saved others, but he can't save himself. If he is the Messiah, the king of Israel, let him come down from the cross! Then we will see and believe.' The two criminals also said cruel things to Jesus.

The Death of Jesus

About noon the sky turned dark and stayed that way until around three o'clock. Then about that time Jesus shouted, '*Eloi, Eloi, lama sabachthani?*' which means, 'My God, my God, why have you deserted me?'

Some of the people standing there heard Jesus and said, 'He is calling for Elijah.' One of them ran and grabbed a sponge. After he had soaked it in wine, he put it on a stick and held it up to Jesus. He said, 'Let's wait and see if Elijah will come and take him down!' Jesus shouted and then died.

At once the curtain* in the temple tore in two from top to bottom.

A Roman army officer was standing in front of Jesus. When the officer saw how Jesus died, he said, 'This man really was the Son of God!'

[*This curtain covers the entrance to the Most Holy Place.]

Mark 16:1–7

Jesus is Alive

After the Sabbath, Mary Magdalene, Salome and Mary the mother of James bought some spices to put on Jesus' body. Very early on Sunday morning, just as the sun was coming up, they went to the tomb. On their way, they were asking one another, 'Who will roll the stone away from the entrance for us?' But when they looked, they saw that the stone had already been rolled away. And it was a huge stone!

The women went into the tomb, and on the right side they saw a young man in a white robe sitting there. They were alarmed.

The man said, 'Don't be alarmed! You are looking for Jesus from Nazareth, who was nailed to a cross. God has raised him to life, and he isn't here. You can see the place where they put his body. Now go and tell his disciples, and especially Peter, that he will go ahead of you to Galilee. You will see him there, just as he told you.'

Luke

This Gospel was almost certainly written by a friend and companion of the apostle Paul, a 'physician' called Luke. He was an educated Gentile from Asia Minor (modern-day Turkey) and wrote in stylish and fluent Greek. He is a particularly gifted storyteller, and it is to him that we owe such wonderful narratives as the 'Good Samaritan' and the 'Prodigal Son', the second of which is included in these extracts from his book. He was also very keen to record the concern of Jesus for the poor, despised or marginalized people in the society of that time – the despised Samaritans, for instance, or the hated 'tax collectors', or the 'lepers', or the women of the streets… or, indeed, women in general, who were regarded mainly as second-class citizens. In many ways, although a man of his time, he was also 'ahead of his time'!

Our other extracts include the temptation of Jesus in the wilderness, Jesus on the cross forgiving his executioners and a penitent thief, and two remarkable stories of his appearances to the disciples after his resurrection.

We begin, however, with Luke's lovely story of the birth of Jesus, the details of which he presumably got from Mary, who went to live with John in Asia Minor after the death of Jesus.

Luke 1:26-38

An Angel Tells About the Birth of Jesus

God sent the angel Gabriel to the town of Nazareth in Galilee with a message for a virgin named Mary. She was engaged to Joseph from the family of King David. The angel greeted Mary and said, 'You are truly blessed! The Lord is with you.'

Mary was confused by the angel's words and wondered what they meant. Then the angel told Mary, 'Don't be afraid! God is pleased with you, and you will have a son. His name will be Jesus. He will be great and will be called the Son of God Most High. The Lord God will make him king, as his ancestor David was. He will rule the people of Israel forever, and his kingdom will never end.'

Mary asked the angel, 'How can this happen? I am not married!'

The angel answered, 'The Holy Spirit will come down to you, and God's power will come over you. So your child will be called the holy Son of God. Your relative Elizabeth is also going to have a son, even though she is old. No one thought she could ever have a baby, but in three months she will have a son. Nothing is impossible for God!'

Mary said, 'I am the Lord's servant! Let it happen as you have said.' And the angel left her.

Luke 2:1–19

The Birth of Jesus

About that time, Emperor Augustus gave orders for the names of all the people to be listed in record books. These first records were made when Quirinius was governor of Syria. Everyone had to go to their own hometown to be listed. So Joseph had to leave Nazareth in Galilee and go to Bethlehem in Judea. Long ago Bethlehem had been King David's hometown, and Joseph went there because he was from David's family.

Mary was engaged to Joseph and travelled with him to Bethlehem. She was soon going to have a baby, and while they were there, she gave birth to her firstborn son. She dressed him in baby clothes and laid him on a bed of hay, because there was no room for them in the inn.

The Shepherds

That night in the fields near Bethlehem, some shepherds were guarding their sheep. All at once an angel came down to them from the Lord, and the brightness of the Lord's glory flashed around them. The shepherds were frightened. But the angel said, 'Don't be afraid! I have good news for you, which will make everyone happy. This very day in King David's hometown a Saviour was born for you. He is Christ the Lord. You will know who he is, because you will find him dressed in baby clothes and lying on a bed of hay.'

Suddenly many other angels came down from heaven and joined in praising God. They said: 'Praise God in heaven! Peace on earth to everyone who pleases God.'

After the angels had left and gone back to heaven, the shepherds said to each other, 'Let's go to Bethlehem and see what the Lord has told us about.' They hurried off and found Mary and Joseph, and they saw the baby lying on a bed of hay.

When the shepherds saw Jesus, they told his parents what the angel had said about him. Everyone listened and was surprised. But Mary kept thinking about all this and wondering what it meant.

Luke 4:1–13

The Temptation of Jesus

When Jesus returned from the Jordan River, the power of the Holy Spirit was with him, and the Spirit led him into the desert. For forty days Jesus was tested by the devil, and during that time he went without eating. When it was all over, he was hungry. The devil said to Jesus, 'If you are God's Son, tell this stone to turn into bread.'

Jesus answered, 'The Scriptures say, "No one can live only on food."'

Then the devil led Jesus up to a high place

and quickly showed him all the nations on earth. The devil said, 'I will give all this power and glory to you. It has been given to me, and I can give it to anyone I want to. Just worship me, and you can have it all.'

Jesus answered, 'The Scriptures say, "Worship the Lord your God and serve only him!"'

Finally, the devil took Jesus to Jerusalem and had him stand on top of the temple. The devil said, 'If you are God's Son, jump off. The Scriptures say, "God will tell his angels to take care of you. They will catch you in their arms, and you will not hurt your feet on the stones."'

Jesus answered, 'The Scriptures also say, "Don't try to test the Lord your God!"'

After the devil had finished testing Jesus in every way possible, he left Jesus for a while.

Luke 15:11–32

Jesus' Story of Two Sons

'Once a man had two sons. The younger son said to his father, "Give me my share of the property." So the father divided his property between his two sons.

'Not long after that, the younger son packed up everything he owned and left for a foreign country, where he wasted all his money in wild living. He had spent everything, when a bad famine spread

through that whole land. Soon he had
nothing to eat.

'He went to work for a man in that
country, and the man sent him out to take
care of his pigs. The son would have been
glad to eat what the pigs were eating, but no
one gave him a thing. Finally, he came to his
senses and said, "My father's workers have
plenty to eat, and here I am, starving to
death! I will go to my father and say to him,
'Father, I have sinned against God in heaven
and against you. I am no longer good enough
to be called your son. Treat me like one of
your workers.'"

'The younger son got up and started back
to his father. But when he was still a long way
off, his father saw him and felt sorry for him.
He ran to his son and hugged and kissed him.

'The son said, "Father, I have sinned
against God in heaven and against you. I am
no longer good enough to be called your
son."

'But his father said to the servants, "Hurry
and bring the best clothes and put them on
him. Give him a ring for his finger and
sandals for his feet. Get the best calf and
prepare it, so we can eat and celebrate. This
son of mine was dead, but has now come
back to life. He was lost and has now been
found." And they began to celebrate.'

The Elder Brother
'The elder son had been out in the field. But
when he came near the house, he heard the

music and dancing. So he called one of the servants over and asked, "What's going on here?"

'The servant answered, "Your brother has come home safe and sound, and your father ordered us to kill the best calf." The older brother got so angry that he would not even go into the house.

'His father came out and begged him to go in. But the elder son said to his father, "For years I have worked for you like a slave and have always obeyed you. But you have never even given me a little goat, so that I could give a dinner for my friends. This son of yours wasted your money on prostitutes. And now that he has come home, you ordered the best calf to be killed for a feast."

'His father replied, "My son, you are always with me, and everything I have is yours. But we should be glad and celebrate! Your brother was dead, but he is now alive. He was lost and has now been found."'

Luke 23:32–43

Jesus on the Cross

Two criminals were led out to be put to death with Jesus. When the soldiers came to the place called 'the Skull', they nailed Jesus to a cross. They also nailed the two criminals to crosses, one on each side of Jesus. Jesus said, 'Father, forgive these people! They don't know what they're doing.' While the crowd stood there watching Jesus, the soldiers gambled for his clothes. The leaders insulted him by saying, 'He saved others. Now he should save himself, if he really is God's chosen Messiah!'

The soldiers made fun of Jesus and brought him some wine. They said, 'If you are the king of the Jews, save yourself!'

Above him was a sign that said, 'This is the King of the Jews.'

One of the criminals hanging there also insulted Jesus by saying, 'Aren't you the Messiah? Save yourself and save us!' But the other criminal told the first one off. 'Don't you fear God? Aren't you getting the same punishment as this man? We got what was coming to us, but he didn't do anything wrong.' Then he said, 'Jesus, remember me when you come into power!'

Jesus replied, 'I promise that today you will be with me in paradise.'

Luke 24:13–40

Easter Day: Jesus Appears to Two Disciples

That same day [the Sunday] two of Jesus' disciples were going to the village of Emmaus, which was about seven miles from Jerusalem. As they were talking and thinking about what had happened, Jesus came near and started walking along beside them. But they did not know who he was.

Jesus asked them, 'What were you talking about as you walked along?'

The two of them stood there looking sad and gloomy. Then the one named Cleopas asked Jesus, 'Are you the only person from Jerusalem who doesn't know what has happened there these last few days?'

'What do you mean?' Jesus asked.

They answered: 'Those things that happened to Jesus from Nazareth. By what he did and said he showed that he was a powerful prophet, who pleased God and all the people. Then the chief priests and our leaders had him arrested and sentenced to die on a cross. We had hoped that he would be the one to set Israel free! But it has already been three days since all this happened. Some women in our group surprised us. They had gone to the tomb early in the morning, but did not find the body of Jesus. They came back, saying that they had seen a vision of angels who told them that he is alive. Some men from our group went to the tomb and found it just as the women had said. But they didn't see Jesus either.'

Then Jesus asked the two disciples, 'Why can't you understand? How can you be so slow to believe all that the prophets said? Didn't you know that the Messiah would have to suffer before he was given his glory?' Jesus then explained everything written about himself in the Scriptures, beginning with the Law of Moses and the Books of the Prophets. When the two of them came near the village where they were going, Jesus seemed to be going further. They begged him, 'Stay with us! It's already late, and the sun is going down.' So Jesus went into the house to stay with them.

After Jesus sat down to eat, he took some bread. He blessed it and broke it. Then he gave it to them. At once they knew who he was, but he disappeared. They said to each other, 'When he talked with us along the road and explained the Scriptures to us, didn't it warm our hearts?' So they got right up and returned to Jerusalem.

The two disciples found the eleven apostles and the others gathered together. And they learned from the group that the Lord was really alive and had appeared to Peter. Then the disciples from Emmaus described what had happened on the road and how they knew he was the Lord when he broke the bread.

Jesus Appears to All the Disciples

While Jesus' disciples were talking about what had happened, Jesus appeared and greeted them. They were frightened and terrified because they thought they were seeing a ghost.

But Jesus said, 'Why are you so frightened? Why do you doubt? Look at my hands and my feet and see who I am! Touch me and find out for yourselves. Ghosts don't have flesh and bones, as you see I have.'

After Jesus said this, he showed them his hands and his feet.

John

John's Gospel is different in style, approach and, in some respects, content from the other three. It's more like a personal 'memoir' written by a close friend quite a long while after the event. It certainly shows the powerful impact that Jesus had on those who knew him best. Our selection includes two miracles (John calls them 'signs') – changing water into wine, and feeding five thousand people with a few small loaves and fishes (the only miracle recorded in each one of the four Gospels). I have included the incident of the woman taken in adultery, even though this story may originally have been found in Luke, and some of the wonderful teaching of Jesus at supper in the upper room on the evening of his betrayal. We end with the moving story of the meeting of Mary Magdalene and the risen Jesus in the garden of the resurrection. Our first extract, though, is the 'prologue', in which Jesus is described as the 'Word' (or 'Explanation') of God.

John 1:1–18

The Word of Life

In the beginning was the one who is called the
Word. The Word was with God and was truly
God. From the very beginning the Word was
with God.

And with this Word, God created all
things.

Nothing was made without the Word.
Everything that was created received its life
from him, and his life gave light to everyone.

The light keeps shining in the dark, and
darkness has never put it out.

God sent a man named John, who came to
tell about the light and to lead all people to
have faith. John wasn't that light. He came
only to tell about the light. The true light that
shines on everyone was coming into the
world.

The Word was in the world, but no one
knew him, though God had made the world
with his Word. He came into his own world,
but his own nation did not welcome him.

Yet some people accepted him and put
their faith in him. So he gave them the right
to be the children of God. They were not
God's children by nature or because of any
human desires. God himself was the one who
made them his children.

The Word became a human being and
lived here with us. We saw his true glory, the
glory of the only Son of the Father. From him

all the kindness and all the truth of God have come down to us.

John spoke about him and cried out, 'This is the one I told you would come! He is greater than I am, because he was alive before I was born.'

Because of all that the Son is, we have been given one blessing after another. The Law was given by Moses, but Jesus Christ brought us undeserved kindness and truth. No one has ever seen God. The only Son, who is truly God and is closest to the Father, has shown us what God is like.

John 2:1–11

Jesus at a Wedding in Cana

Mary, the mother of Jesus, was at a wedding feast in the village of Cana in Galilee. Jesus and his disciples had also been invited and were there.

When the wine was all gone, Mary said to Jesus, 'They don't have any more wine.'

Jesus replied, 'Mother, my time hasn't yet come: you must not tell me what to do.' Mary then said to the servants, 'Do whatever Jesus tells you to do.'

At the feast there were six stone water jars that were used by the people for washing themselves in the way that their religion said they must. Each jar held about twenty or thirty gallons. Jesus told the servants to fill them to the top with water. Then, after the jars had been filled, he said, 'Now take some water and give it to the man in charge of the feast.'

The servants did as Jesus told them, and the man in charge drank some of the water that had now turned into wine. He did not know where the wine had come from, but the servants did. The man called the bridegroom over and said, 'The best wine is usually served first. Then after the guests have had plenty, the other wine is served. But you have kept the best until last!'

This was Jesus' first sign, and he did it in the village of Cana in Galilee. There Jesus showed his glory, and his disciples put their faith in him.

John 6:1–21, 24–35

Feeding the Five Thousand

Jesus crossed Lake Galilee, which was also known as Lake Tiberias. A large crowd had seen him work miracles to heal the sick, and those people went with him. It was almost time for the Jewish festival of Passover, and Jesus went up on a mountain with his disciples and sat down. When Jesus saw the large crowd coming towards him, he asked Philip, 'Where will we get enough food to feed all these people?' He said this to test Philip, since he already knew what he was going to do.

Philip answered, 'Don't you know that it would take almost a year's wages just to buy only a little bread for each of these people?' Andrew, the brother of Simon Peter, was one of the disciples. He spoke up and said, 'There is a boy here who has five small loaves of barley bread and two fish. But what good is that with all these people?' The ground was covered with grass, and Jesus told his disciples to have everyone sit down. About five thousand men were in the crowd. Jesus took the bread in his hands and gave thanks to God. Then he passed the bread to the people, and he did the same with the fish, until everyone had plenty to eat.

The people ate all they wanted, and Jesus told his disciples to gather up the leftovers, so that nothing would be wasted. The disciples gathered them up and filled twelve large baskets with what was left over from the five barley loaves.

After the people had seen Jesus work this miracle, they began saying, 'This must be the Prophet who is to come into the world!' Jesus realized that they would try to force him to be their king. So he went up on a mountain, where he could be alone.

Jesus Walks on the Water

That evening, Jesus' disciples went down to the lake. They got into a boat and started across for Capernaum. Later that evening Jesus had still not come to them, and a strong wind was making the water rough.

When the disciples had rowed for three or four miles, they saw Jesus walking on the water. He kept coming closer to the boat, and they were terrified. But he said, 'I am Jesus! Don't be afraid!' The disciples wanted to take him into the boat, but suddenly the boat reached the shore where they were headed.

The Bread That Gives Life

The people saw that Jesus and his disciples had left. Then they got into the boats and went to Capernaum to look for Jesus. They found him on the west side of the lake and asked, 'Rabbi, when did you get here?'

Jesus answered, 'I tell you for certain that you are not looking for me because you saw the miracles, but because you ate all the food you wanted. Don't work for food that spoils. Work for food that gives eternal life. The Son of Man will give you this food, because God the Father has given him the right to do so.'

'What exactly does God want us to do?' the people asked.

Jesus answered, 'God wants you to have faith in the one he sent.'

They replied, 'What miracle will you work, so that we can have faith in you? What will you do? For example, when our ancestors were in the desert, they were given manna to eat. It happened just as the Scriptures say: "God gave them bread from heaven to eat."' Jesus then told them, 'I tell you for certain that Moses wasn't the one who gave you bread from heaven. My Father is the one who gives you the true bread from heaven. And the bread that God gives is the one who came down from heaven to give life to the world.'

The people said, 'Lord, give us this bread and don't ever stop!'

Jesus replied, 'I am the bread that gives life! No one who comes to me will ever be hungry. No one who has faith in me will ever be thirsty.'

John 8:2–11

The Woman Caught in the Act of Adultery

Early the next morning Jesus went to the temple. The people came to him, and he sat down and started teaching them. The Pharisees and the teachers of the Law of Moses brought in a woman who had been caught in the act of adultery with a man who wasn't her husband. They made her stand in the middle of the crowd. Then they said, 'Teacher, this woman was caught in the act of adultery. The Law of Moses teaches that a woman like this should be stoned to death! What do you say?'

They asked Jesus this question, because they wanted to test him and bring some charge against him. But Jesus simply bent over and started writing on the ground with his finger.

They kept on asking Jesus about the

woman. Finally, he stood up and said, 'If any of you has never sinned, then go ahead and throw the first stone at her!' Once again he bent over and began writing on the ground. The people left one by one, beginning with the oldest. Finally, Jesus and the woman were there alone.

Jesus stood up and asked her, 'Where is everyone? Isn't there anyone left to accuse you?'

'No sir,' the woman answered.

Then Jesus told her, 'I am not going to accuse you either. You may go now, but don't sin any more.'

John 10:1–16

A Story About Sheep

Jesus said, 'I tell you for certain that only thieves and robbers climb over the fence instead of going in through the gate to the sheep pen. But the gatekeeper opens the gate for the shepherd, and he goes in through it. The sheep know their shepherd's voice. He calls each of them by name and leads them out. When he has led out all of his sheep, he walks in front of them, and they follow, because they know his voice. The sheep will not follow strangers. They don't recognize a stranger's voice, and they run away.'

Jesus told the people this story. But they did not understand what he was talking about.

Jesus is the Good Shepherd

Jesus said, 'I tell you for certain that I am the gate for the sheep. Everyone who came before me was a thief or a robber, and the sheep did not listen to any of them. I am the gate. All who come in through me will be saved. Through me they will come and go and find pasture. A thief comes only to rob, kill and destroy. I came so that everyone would have life, and have it in its fullest. I am the good shepherd, and the good shepherd gives up his life for his sheep. Hired workers are not like the shepherd. They don't own the sheep, and when they see a wolf coming, they run off and leave the sheep. Then the wolf attacks and scatters the flock. Hired workers run away because they don't care about the sheep.

'I am the good shepherd. I know my sheep, and they know me. Just as the Father knows me, I know the Father, and I give up my life for my sheep. I have other sheep that are not in this sheep pen. I must bring them together too, when they hear my voice. Then there will be one flock of sheep and one shepherd.'

John 14:1–17

In the Upper Room: Jesus is the Way to the Father

Jesus said to his disciples, 'Don't be worried! Have faith in God and have faith in me. There are many rooms in my Father's house. I wouldn't tell you this, unless it was true. I am going there to prepare a place for each of you. After I have done this, I will come back and take you with me. Then we will be together. You know the way to where I am going.'

Thomas said, 'Lord, we don't even know where you are going! How can we know the way?'

'I am the way, the truth and the life!' Jesus answered. 'Without me, no one can go to the Father. If you had known me, you would have known the Father. But from now on, you do know him, and you have seen him.'

Philip said, 'Lord, show us the Father. That is all we need.'

Jesus replied, 'Philip, I have been with you for a long time. Don't you know who I am? If you have seen me, you have seen the Father. How can you ask me to show you the Father? Don't you believe that I am one with the Father and that the Father is one with me? What I say isn't said on my own. The Father who lives in me does these things.

'Have faith in me when I say that the Father is one with me and that I am one with the Father. Or else have faith in me simply because of the things I do. I tell you for certain that if you have faith in me, you will do the same things that I am doing. You will do even greater things, now that I am going back to the Father. Ask me, and I will do whatever you ask. This way the Son will bring honour to the Father. I will do whatever you ask me to do.'

The Holy Spirit is Promised

Jesus said to his disciples, 'If you love me, you will do as I command. Then I will ask the Father to send you the Holy Spirit who will help you and will always be with you. The Spirit will show you what is true. The people of this world cannot accept the Spirit, because they don't see or know him. But you know the Spirit, who is with you and will keep on living in you.'

John 20:11–18

Easter Morning: Jesus Appears to Mary Magdalene

Mary Magdalene was crying outside the tomb. She was still weeping when she stooped down and saw two angels inside. They were dressed in white and were sitting where Jesus' body had been. One was at the head and the other was at the foot. The angels asked Mary, 'Why are you crying?'

She answered, 'They have taken away my Lord's body! I don't know where they have put him.'

As soon as Mary said this, she turned around and saw Jesus standing there. But she did not know who he was. Jesus asked her, 'Why are you crying? Who are you looking for?'

She thought he was the gardener and said, 'Sir, if you have taken his body away, please tell me, so I can go and get him.'

Then Jesus said to her, 'Mary!'

She turned and said to him, '*Rabboni*.'*
Jesus told her, 'Don't hold on to me! I have not
yet gone to the Father. But tell my disciples
that I am going to the one who is my Father
and my God, as well as your Father and your
God.' Mary Magdalene then went and told
the disciples that she had seen the Lord. She
also told them what he had said to her.

[*The Aramaic word '*Rabboni*' means teacher.]

Acts of the Apostles

This is a second book by Luke, recording
the story of the emerging church from the
time of the resurrection of Jesus to its
establishment through much of the Roman
world. Our extracts are the accounts of the
ascension of Jesus (his return to the Father
in heaven) and of the special gift of the
Holy Spirit to the apostles at the feast of
Pentecost, forty days later. Finally there is
the dramatic story of the conversion of Saul
of Tarsus (who was renamed Paul) on the
road to Damascus.

Acts 1:6–12

Jesus is Taken to Heaven

While the apostles were still with Jesus, they asked him, 'Lord, are you now going to give Israel its own king again?' Jesus said to them, 'You don't need to know the time of those events that only the Father controls. But the Holy Spirit will come upon you and give you power. Then you will tell everyone about me in Jerusalem, in all Judea, in Samaria and everywhere in the world.' After Jesus had said this and while they were watching, he was taken up into a cloud. They could not see him, but as he went up, they kept looking up into the sky.

Suddenly two men dressed in white clothes were standing there beside them. They said, 'Why are you men from Galilee standing here and looking up into the sky? Jesus has been taken to heaven. But he will come back in the same way that you have seen him go.'

Acts 2:1–24, 31–42

The Coming of the Holy Spirit

On the day of Pentecost, all the Lord's followers were together in one place. Suddenly there was a noise from heaven like the sound of a mighty wind! It filled the house where they were meeting. Then they saw what looked like fiery tongues moving in all directions, and a tongue came and settled on each person there. The Holy Spirit took control of everyone, and they began speaking whatever languages the Spirit let them speak. Many religious Jews from every country in the world were living in Jerusalem. And when they heard this noise, a crowd gathered. But they were surprised, because they were hearing everything in their own languages. They were excited and amazed, and said:

'Don't all these who are speaking come from Galilee? Then why do we hear them speaking our very own languages? Some of us are from Parthia, Media and Elam. Others are from Mesopotamia, Judea, Cappadocia, Pontus, Asia, Phrygia, Pamphylia, Egypt, parts of Libya near Cyrene, Rome, Crete and Arabia. Some of us were born Jews, and others of us have chosen to be Jews. Yet we all hear them using our own languages to tell the wonderful things God has done.'

Everyone was excited and confused. Some of them even kept asking each other, 'What does all this mean?'

Others made fun of the Lord's followers and said, 'They are drunk.'

Peter Speaks to the Crowd

Peter stood with the eleven apostles and spoke in a loud and clear voice to the crowd:

'Friends and everyone else living in Jerusalem, listen carefully to what I have to say! You are wrong to think that these people are drunk. After all, it is only nine o'clock in the morning. But this is what God had the prophet Joel say, "When the last days come, I will give my Spirit to everyone. Your sons and daughters will prophesy.

"Your young men will see visions, and your old men will have dreams. In those days I will give my Spirit to my servants, both men and women, and they will prophesy.

"I will work miracles in the sky above and wonders on the earth below. There will be blood and fire and clouds of smoke. The sun will turn dark, and the moon will be as red as blood before the great and wonderful day of the Lord appears. Then the Lord will save everyone who asks for his help."

'Now, listen to what I have to say about Jesus from Nazareth. God proved that he sent Jesus to you by having him work miracles, wonders and signs. All of you know this. God had already planned and decided that Jesus would be handed over to you. So you took him and had evil men put him to death on a cross. But God set him free from death and raised him to life. Death could not hold him in its power... David knew this would happen, and so he told us that Christ would be raised to life. He said that God would not leave him in the grave or let his body decay. All of us can tell you that God has raised Jesus to life! Jesus was taken up to sit at the right side of God, and he was given the Holy Spirit, just as the Father had promised. Jesus is also the one who has given the Spirit to us, and that is what you are now seeing and hearing. David didn't go up to heaven. So he wasn't talking about himself when he said, "The Lord told my Lord to sit at his right side, until he made my Lord's enemies into a footstool for him." Everyone in Israel should then know for certain that God has made Jesus both Lord and Christ, even though you put him to death on a cross.'

When the people heard this, they were very upset. They asked Peter and the other apostles, 'Friends, what shall we do?'

Peter said, 'Turn back to God! Be baptized in the name of Jesus Christ, so that your sins will be forgiven. Then you will be given the Holy Spirit. This promise is for you and your children. It is for everyone our Lord God will choose, no matter where they live.'

Peter told them many other things as well. Then he said, 'I beg you to save yourselves from this corrupt generation.' On that day about three thousand believed his message and were baptized. They spent their time learning from the apostles, and they were like family to each other. They also broke bread and prayed together.

Acts 9:1–19

The Damascus Road

Saul kept on threatening to kill the Lord's followers. He even went to the high priest and asked for letters to the Jewish leaders in Damascus. He did this because he wanted to arrest and take to Jerusalem any man or woman who had accepted the Lord's Way. When Saul had almost reached Damascus, a bright light from heaven suddenly flashed around him. He fell to the ground and heard a voice that said, 'Saul! Saul! Why are you so cruel to me?'

'Who are you?' Saul asked.

'I am Jesus,' the Lord answered. 'I am the one you are so cruel to. Now get up and go into the city, where you will be told what to do.'

The men with Saul stood there speechless. They had heard the voice, but they had not seen anyone. Saul got up from the ground, and when he opened his eyes, he could not see a thing. Someone then led him by the hand to Damascus, and for three days he was blind and did not eat or drink.

A follower named Ananias lived in Damascus, and the Lord spoke to him in a vision. Ananias answered, 'Lord, here I am.'

The Lord said to him, 'Get up and go to the house of Judas on Straight Street. When you get there, you will find a man named Saul from the city of Tarsus. Saul is praying, and he has seen a vision. He saw a man named Ananias coming to him and putting his hands on him, so that he could see again.'

Ananias replied, 'Lord, a lot of people have told me about the terrible things this man has done to your followers in Jerusalem. Now the chief priests have given him the power to come here and arrest anyone who worships in your name.'

The Lord said to Ananias, 'Go! I have chosen him to tell foreigners, kings and the people of Israel about me. I will show him how much he must suffer for worshipping in my name.'

Ananias left and went into the house where Saul was staying. Ananias placed his hands on him and said, 'Saul, the Lord Jesus has sent me. He is the same one who appeared to you along the road. He wants you to be able to see and to be filled with the Holy Spirit.'

Suddenly something like fish scales fell from Saul's eyes, and he could see. He got up and was baptized.* Then he ate and felt much better. For several days Saul stayed with the Lord's followers in Damascus.

[*After his baptism, Saul was known as 'Paul' and eventually became the great missionary to the Gentile nations.]

The Epistles

Most of the rest of the New Testament is occupied by what are known as the epistles – letters sent in the name of various Christian leaders to the churches that were being formed throughout the Roman empire. Most are from Paul – an inveterate correspondent – but there are also letters by James, John, Peter and others. They were intended to guide, advise, direct, teach and encourage these groups of new Christians in their faith. I have selected three well-known passages from Paul's letters (to the churches at Rome, Corinth and Philippi), and one each from letters by Peter and John.

Romans 8:31–39

'Nothing can Separate Us from God's Love'

What can we say about all this? If God is on our side, can anyone be against us? God did not keep back his own Son, but he gave him for us. If God did this, won't he freely give us everything else? If God says his chosen ones are acceptable to him, can anyone bring charges against them? Or can anyone condemn them? No indeed! Christ died and was raised to life, and now he is at

God's right side, speaking to him for us.
Can anything separate us from the love of
Christ? Can trouble, suffering and hard
times, or hunger and nakedness, or danger
and death? It is exactly as the Scriptures
say: 'For you we face death all day long.
We are like sheep on their way to be
butchered.'

In everything we have won more than a
victory because of Christ who loves us. I am
sure that nothing can separate us from God's
love – not life or death, not angels or spirits,
not the present or the future, and not powers
above or powers below. Nothing in all creation
can separate us from God's love for us in
Christ Jesus our Lord!

1 Corinthians 13:1–13

Love Never Ends
What if I could speak all languages of
humans and of angels?

If I did not love others, I would be
nothing more than a noisy gong or a
clanging cymbal.

What if I could prophesy and understand
all secrets and all knowledge?

And what if I had faith that moved
mountains?

I would be nothing, unless I loved others.

What if I gave away all that I owned and let myself be burned alive?

I would gain nothing, unless I loved others.

Love is kind and patient, never jealous, boastful, proud or rude.

Love isn't selfish or quick-tempered. It doesn't keep a record of wrongs that others do.

Love rejoices in the truth, but not in evil.

Love is always supportive, loyal, hopeful and trusting.

Love never fails!

Everyone who prophesies will stop, and unknown languages will no longer be spoken.

All that we know will be forgotten. We don't know everything, and our prophecies are not complete.

But what is perfect will someday appear, and what isn't perfect will then disappear.

When we were children, we thought and reasoned as children do.

But when we grew up, we gave up our childish ways.

Now all we can see of God is like a cloudy picture in a mirror.

Later we will see him face to face.

We don't know everything, but then we will, just as God completely understands us.

For now there are faith, hope and love.

But of these three, the greatest is love.

Philippians 2:5–11

A Christ-like Mind

Think the same way that Christ Jesus thought:

Christ was truly God.

But he did not try to remain equal with God.

Instead he gave up everything and became
a slave, when he became like one of us.

Christ was humble.

He obeyed God and even died on a cross.

Then God gave Christ the highest place
and honoured his name above all others.

So at the name of Jesus everyone will bow
down, those in heaven, on earth and under
the earth.

And to the glory of God the Father,
everyone will openly agree, 'Jesus Christ is
Lord!'

1 Peter 1:3–9

New Life, New Hope, New Joy

Praise God, the Father of our Lord Jesus
Christ. God is so good, and by raising Jesus
from death, he has given us new life and a
hope that lives on. God has something stored
up for you in heaven, where it will never
decay or be ruined or disappear.

You have faith in God, whose power will
protect you until the last day. Then he will
save you, just as he has always planned to do.

On that day you will be glad, even if you have to go through many hard trials for a while. Your faith will be like gold that has been tested in a fire. And these trials will prove that your faith is worth much more than gold, which can be destroyed. They will show that you will be given praise and honour and glory when Jesus Christ returns. You have never seen Jesus, and you don't see him now. But still you love him and have faith in him, and no words can tell how glad and happy you are to be saved. That's why you have faith.

1 John 4:7–21

God is Love

My dear friends, we must love each other. Love comes from God, and when we love each other, it shows that we have been given new life. We are now God's children, and we know him. God is love, and anyone who doesn't love others has never known him. God showed his love for us when he sent his only Son into the world to give us life. Real love isn't our love for God, but his love for us. God sent his Son to be the sacrifice by which our sins are forgiven. Dear friends, since God loved us this much, we must love each other.

No one has ever seen God. But if we love each other, God lives in us, and his love is truly in our hearts.

God has given us his Spirit. That is how we know that we are one with him, just as he is one with us. God sent his Son to be the Saviour of the world. We saw his Son and are now telling others about him. God stays one with everyone who openly says that Jesus is the Son of God. That's how we stay one with God and are sure that God loves us.

God is love. If we keep on loving others, we will stay one in our hearts with God, and he will stay one with us. If we truly love others and live as Christ did in this world, we won't be worried about the day of judgment. A real love for others will chase those worries away. The thought of being punished is what makes us afraid. It shows that we have not really learned to love.

We love because God loved us first. But if we say we love God and don't love each other, we are liars. We cannot see God. So how can we love God, if we don't love the people we can see? The commandment that God has given us is: 'Love God and love each other!'

Revelation

The Bible ends with a remarkable series of visions given to a man called John on the island of Patmos while he was 'in the spirit'.

Its literary genre is called 'apocalyptic', which means 'uncovered' – a kind of coded message for those who are initiated. Although this book has been a happy hunting ground for cranks and number crunchers, its fundamental message is in line with the whole story of the Bible. Whatever happens, whatever disaster or persecution comes, God is still 'on the throne' and one day his purposes of justice and love will be fulfilled. Our extract is from the end of the book – a wonderful vision of the City of God.

Revelation 21:1–7

A Vision of Heaven

I saw a new heaven and a new earth. The first heaven and the first earth had disappeared, and so had the sea. Then I saw New Jerusalem, that holy city, coming down from God in heaven. It was like a bride dressed in her wedding gown and ready to meet her husband.

I heard a loud voice shout from the throne: 'God's home is now with his people. He will live with them, and they will be his own. Yes, God will make his home among his people. He will wipe all tears from their eyes, and there will be no more death, suffering, crying or pain. These things of the past are gone forever.'

Then the one sitting on the throne said: 'I am making everything new. Write down what I have said. My words are true and can be trusted. Everything is finished! I am Alpha and Omega, the beginning and the end. I will freely give water from the life-giving fountain to everyone who is thirsty. All who win the victory will be given these blessings. I will be their God, and they will be my people.'

The Last Word

So *The Espresso Bible* ends with a vision of perfect bliss – peace, harmony, joy and contentment in a new society where God and humanity can live together in perfect unity of mind and heart. Thus, at the end of the Bible's story, the tragedy of the rebellion in the Garden of Eden is reversed. Men and women are back in the 'garden of delight'. Sin and failure have been forgiven through the death of Jesus, the 'Lamb of God'. The One who made everything 'new' at the original creation has done it again! There is a new world, a new hope, a new way of living.